EMINENT DOMAIN
AND LOCAL GOVERNMENT IN NORTH CAROLINA
LAW AND PROCEDURE

UNC
SCHOOL OF GOVERNMENT

EMINENT DOMAIN
AND LOCAL GOVERNMENT IN NORTH CAROLINA
LAW AND PROCEDURE

first edition
Charles Szypszak

UNC
SCHOOL OF GOVERNMENT

The School of Government at the University of North Carolina at Chapel Hill works to improve the lives of North Carolinians by engaging in practical scholarship that helps public officials and citizens understand and strengthen state and local government. Established in 1931 as the Institute of Government, the School provides educational, advisory, and research services for state and local governments. The School of Government is also home to a nationally ranked graduate program in public administration and specialized centers focused on information technology, environmental finance, and civic education for youth.

As the largest university-based local government training, advisory, and research organization in the United States, the School of Government offers up to 200 classes, seminars, schools, and specialized conferences for more than 12,000 public officials each year. In addition, faculty members annually publish approximately fifty books, periodicals, and other reference works related to state and local government. Each day that the General Assembly is in session, the School produces the *Daily Bulletin*, which reports on the day's activities for members of the legislature and others who need to follow the course of legislation.

The Master of Public Administration Program is a full-time, two-year program that serves up to sixty students annually. It consistently ranks among the best public administration graduate programs in the country, particularly in city management. With courses ranging from public policy analysis to ethics and management, the program educates leaders for local, state, and federal governments and nonprofit organizations.

Operating support for the School of Government's programs and activities comes from many sources, including state appropriations, local government membership dues, private contributions, publication sales, course fees, and service contracts. Visit www.sog.unc.edu or call 919.966.5381 for more information on the School's courses, publications, programs, and services.

Michael R. Smith, DEAN
Thomas H. Thornburg, SENIOR ASSOCIATE DEAN
Frayda S. Bluestein, ASSOCIATE DEAN FOR PROGRAMS
Todd A. Nicolet, ASSOCIATE DEAN FOR INFORMATION TECHNOLOGY
Ann Cary Simpson, ASSOCIATE DEAN FOR DEVELOPMENT AND COMMUNICATIONS
Bradley G. Volk, ASSOCIATE DEAN FOR ADMINISTRATION

FACULTY

Gregory S. Allison	Cheryl Daniels Howell	William C. Rivenbark
Stephen Allred (on leave)	Joseph E. Hunt	Dale J. Roenigk
David N. Ammons	Willow S. Jacobson	John Rubin
Ann M. Anderson	Robert P. Joyce	John L. Saxon
A. Fleming Bell, II	Kenneth L. Joyner	Shannon H. Schelin
Maureen M. Berner	Diane M. Juffras	Jessica Smith
Mark F. Botts	David M. Lawrence	Karl W. Smith
Joan G. Brannon	Dona G. Lewandowski	Carl W. Stenberg III
Molly C. Broad	James M. Markham	John B. Stephens
Michael Crowell	Janet Mason	Charles Szypszak
Shea Riggsbee Denning	Laurie L. Mesibov	Vaughn Upshaw
James C. Drennan	Kara A. Millonzi	A. John Vogt
Richard D. Ducker	Jill D. Moore	Aimee N. Wall
Robert L. Farb	Jonathan Q. Morgan	Jeff Welty
Joseph S. Ferrell	Ricardo S. Morse	Richard B. Whisnant
Milton S. Heath Jr.	Tyler Mulligan	Gordon P. Whitaker
Norma Houston (on leave)	David W. Owens	Eileen Youens

© 2008

School of Government

The University of North Carolina at Chap el Hill

First edition 2008.

Printed in the United States of America

Cover photo by Callie Barber

12 11 10 09 08   1 2 3 4 5

ISBN 978-1-56011-573-1

♾ This publication is printed on permanent, acid-free paper in compliance with the North Carolina General Statutes.

♻ Printed on recycled paper

Contents

Acknowledgments   vii

Introduction   ix

1   **Local Government Eminent Domain Powers**   1

     1.1   The Nature of Eminent Domain   3

     1.2   Origins of Eminent Domain Power   4

     1.3   Public Use and Benefit   10

     1.4   Owner's Right to Compensation   19

     1.5   Rights Subject to Eminent Domain   21

     1.6   Authority to Determine Property Needed   24

     1.7   Chapter 40A Eminent Domain Powers of Municipalities and Counties   26

     1.8   Other Local Public Authorities with Eminent Domain Powers under Chapter 40A   31

     1.9   Other Local Government Authorities Having Eminent Domain Powers   36

     1.10   Eminent Domain Power Conferred by Local Acts   39

     1.11   Cross-Jurisdictional Eminent Domain   42

2   **Local Government Eminent Domain Procedure**   43

     2.1   Overview and Practice Considerations   45

     2.2   Offer to Purchase or Request for Gift   47

     2.3   Dispute Resolution Forum   47

     2.4   Rules of Litigation Procedure   50

     2.5   Vesting of Title; Injunctive Relief   51

     2.6   Parties to Eminent Domain Action   54

     2.7   Discovery and Proof of Value   59

     2.8   Pleadings, Notices, and Other Litigation Requirements   64

     2.9   Abandonment of Project during Proceeding   83

     2.10   Judgment and Payment of Compensation   84

     2.11   Costs and Attorneys' Fees   92

     2.12   Return of Condemned Property   92

     2.13   Inverse Condemnation Procedure   93

3   Just Compensation   95

3.1   Fair Market Value   97

3.2   Valuation Methods   99

3.3   Date as to Which Value Is Measured   101

3.4   Valuation of Partial Takings   102

3.5   Effect of Public Improvements   102

3.6   Affected Property   107

3.7   Several Interests and Extraction Rights   109

3.8   Loss of Business Income   111

3.9   Easements   113

3.10   Leases   115

3.11   Life Estates   116

3.12   Real Estate Liens   117

3.13   Relocation Assistance   118

3.14   Interest   120

4   Inverse Condemnation   123

4.1   Origins and Nature of Inverse Condemnation   125

4.2   Statutory Remedy for Local Government Inverse
       Condemnation   127

4.3   Inverse Condemnation for Physical Intrusions   134

4.4   Inverse Condemnation for Changes Affecting Access   141

4.5   Regulatory Takings   144

Index   153

Acknowledgments

This book benefited from the contributions of scholars, practitioners, researchers, and editors. Special acknowledgment is due to Raleigh Deputy City Attorney Francis (Razz) Rasberry, who shared his extensive experience, considerable expertise, and practitioner's perspective and provided many thoughtful comments and suggestions. Thanks also to Professor David Lawrence, whose extraordinary breadth of knowledge afforded astute insights that clarified and improved analytical material. Associate Dean and Professor Frayda Bluestein made perceptive suggestions and provided encouragement throughout the project. John King, a student in the Master of Public Administration Program at the School of Government, conducted valuable research in connection with the material addressing procedure.

With all projects at the School of Government, current faculty profit from the groundwork laid by those formerly associated with the School and Institute of Government and the reputation they earned for reliable, objective analysis. This book follows two editions of a guidebook entitled *Eminent Domain Procedure for North Carolina Local Governments* by Professor Ben F. Loeb Jr., and his work was preceded by a guide entitled *Eminent Domain Powers of Cities and Counties* by Robert E. Phay, former assistant director of the Institute of Government.

Credit also is due to practitioners who present eminent domain cases clearly, fairly, and ultimately in the public interest. Many of the forms and comments in this book reflect the professionalism and good work of these practitioners.

Charles Szypszak
Associate Professor of Public Law and Government

Introduction

North Carolina's local government officials often must acquire property for essential public improvements, and owners of needed property are not always willing to transfer it voluntarily. Owners may face the prospect of having to relinquish property for public improvements in exchange for what the law defines as "just compensation." This book is primarily intended to provide local government officials and their attorneys an overview of the complex area of the law known as eminent domain, as it has been addressed in North Carolina's statutes and interpreted and applied by the courts, and basic guidance concerning the required procedures. This book should also provide insight to property owners seeking a better understanding of eminent domain and serve as a useful resource for judges and lawmakers who consider eminent domain law and procedure and prospects for their refinement.

Chapter 1 discusses the nature of eminent domain and its evolution in North Carolina law and the extent of eminent domain authority currently entrusted to local governments and their instrumentalities. Chapter 2 addresses the procedure local governments must follow as they acquire property through an eminent domain process. Chapter 3 discusses the just compensation that must be paid to owners and how the amount of that compensation is determined. Chapter 4 discusses inverse condemnation, which occurs when a government takes or uses property without first following the eminent domain procedure.

The statutes governing eminent domain law and procedure are subject to change every time the General Assembly convenes. And more so than with many areas of the law, the courts' approaches to difficult interpretive issues involving eminent domain change over time, and these outcomes tend to be contextual. Some of the discussion in this book required reconciliation of statutory provisions and judicial interpretations that do not always fit neatly together. Although every effort was made to provide a reliable resource, there is room for disagreement about the subjects discussed in this book, and those involved in eminent domain matters ultimately must rely on their own research and judgment.

EMINENT DOMAIN
AND LOCAL GOVERNMENT IN NORTH CAROLINA
LAW AND PROCEDURE

1   Local Government Eminent Domain Powers

1.1   **The Nature of Eminent Domain**   3

1.2   **Origins of Eminent Domain Power**   4

    1.2.1   Eminent Domain in the Republic   5

    1.2.2   Evolution of Eminent Domain Law in North Carolina   6

1.3   **Public Use and Benefit**   10

    1.3.1   United States Supreme Court on Permissible Eminent Domain   10

    1.3.2   North Carolina Law on Permissible Eminent Domain   11

    1.3.3   Review of Extent of Legislative Authorization   18

1.4   **Owner's Right to Compensation**   19

1.5   **Rights Subject to Eminent Domain**   21

1.6   **Authority to Determine Property Needed**   24

1.7   **Chapter 40A Eminent Domain Powers of Municipalities and Counties**   26

    1.7.1   All Municipalities and Counties   27

    1.7.2   Municipalities   29

    1.7.3   Counties   29

    1.7.4   Coastal Counties and Municipalities   30

1.8   **Other Local Public Authorities with Eminent Domain Powers under Chapter 40A**   31

    1.8.1   Community College Trustees   31

    1.8.2   Federal Housing Projects   31

    1.8.3   Hospital Authorities   31

    1.8.4   Housing Authorities   32

    1.8.5   Mosquito Control Districts   32

    1.8.6   Regional Public Transportation Authorities   33

1.8.7   Sanitary District Boards   33

1.8.8   School Boards   33

1.8.9   Urban Redevelopment Commissions   34

1.8.10   Water and Sewer Local Government Organizations   34

1.8.11   Watershed Improvement Districts   35

1.9   Other Local Government Authorities Having Eminent Domain Powers   36

1.9.1   Joint Municipal Electrical Power Projects   36

1.9.2   Public Landings   36

1.9.3   Public Transportation Authorities   37

1.9.4   Regional Natural Gas Districts   37

1.9.5   Regional Solid Waste Management Authorities   37

1.9.6   Revenue Bond Projects   38

1.9.7   Special Airport Districts   38

1.9.8   State Highway System Streets   38

1.10   Eminent Domain Power Conferred by Local Acts   39

1.11   Cross-Jurisdictional Eminent Domain   42

1.1   The Nature of Eminent Domain

Eminent domain ranks with war and taxation among the most emotionally charged of all government powers. Some consider the compelled transfer of private property to government authorities the kind of oppressive act in response to which the revolutionary founders declared independence from their colonial government. Despite the potential volatility of the eminent domain power, its legal legitimacy for use by a representative government to acquire property for roads and other essential public facilities has never been seriously challenged. This may seem paradoxical, because the United States and North Carolina constitutions do not mention eminent domain among the powers entrusted to government. Legal authorities have interpreted this quiescence as a reflection of the power's assumed existence rather than as an intent to withhold such power from the newly formed governments. The assumption persisted from colonial times through the creation of new state and federal governments and thereafter and is implicit in actions and decisions of federal and state legislators, executive officers, and judges who make laws, administer government, and resolve disputes.

Although the founders did not expressly confirm the existence of a power of eminent domain in foundational legal documents, they did refer to constraints on its legitimate purpose and use. The federal and state constitutions have been interpreted as requiring that eminent domain be employed only for public use or benefit and only when owners receive just compensation for the property taken from them. Although the power of eminent domain has not been seriously challenged, the nature of the constraints on its exercise has been the subject of much legislation, judicial interpretation, debate, and sometimes outrage.

This book concerns the North Carolina state government's eminent domain power as the North Carolina General Assembly has delegated it to local governments, including the purposes for which it can be exercised lawfully, the court procedures that must be followed when it is employed, and the nature of the compensation that must be paid to owners from whom property is acquired. It addresses the essential legal issues. However, local governments contemplating use of eminent domain also must remember that legal authority is not the only factor to consider when deciding whether to wield a particular power. Local governments often have the alternative of acquiring property by agreement with the owner the same as any other potential purchaser. But owners are not always reasonable in their expectations, and sometimes a public project is so complex that it is not feasible without the use of eminent domain, or at least the potential that the power could be used.[1]

Eminent domain puts the government and individual citizens in conflict. Public officials are compelling surrender of private property in the name of the greater public interest. Owners must surrender that property in exchange for what will be determined to be just compensation. Those responsible for initiating and managing the government action are in the best position to make a compelling case for acquiring the property in a way that will minimize conflict. As Thomas Jefferson once said regarding taking private property for public use: "As tedious as is the operation of reasoning with every individual on whom we are obliged to exercise disagreeable powers, yet free people think they have a right to an explanation of the circumstances which give rise to the necessity under which they suffer."[2] Owners who can see the public benefits of the project for which their property is being acquired and who are treated fairly are less likely to refuse good faith offers or to oppose the project. Public administrators and their counsel advance their service to the public by being mindful of such reasonable expectations.

1.2   Origins of Eminent Domain Power

The phrase "eminent domain" refers to the state's power to take property from private owners for public use or benefit.[3] The phrase is attributed to the Dutch legal philosopher Hugo Grotius, who in 1625 described the following government prerogative: "The property of subjects is under the eminent

---

1. Consider, for example, the daunting scope of the Randleman Reservoir project in Guilford and Randolph counties, which will provide forty-eight million gallons of water a day, and the construction of which has spanned decades and involves hundreds of parcels. Most of the necessary property rights were obtained by agreement with the owners, but eminent domain was deemed necessary in over 100 instances, as indicated by the records in the county offices of the registers of deeds. *See generally* Piedmont Triad Regional Water Authority, History of Randleman Lake, www.ptrwa.org/history.htm (last visited March 27, 2008) (discussing the history of the reservoir project).

2. Letter from Thomas Jefferson to Nathanael Greene (Apr. 5, 1781), *reprinted in* 5 PAPERS OF THOMAS JEFFERSON 356 (Julian P. Boyd ed., 1952).

3. 1 JULIUS L. SACKMAN, NICHOLS ON EMINENT DOMAIN § 1.12[1] (3d ed. 2007).

domain of the State, so that the State, or he who acts for it, may use and even alienate and destroy such property, not only in case of extreme necessity, in which even private persons have a right over the property of others, but for ends of public utility, to which ends those who founded civil society must be supposed to have intended that private ends should give way."[4] Exercise of this power is sometimes referred to as "condemnation," which derives from the act of exacting something from a landowner, or a "taking," which refers to the compulsion by which the government acquires private property by use of this power.

As the next sections describe, the eminent domain power was firmly embedded in legal thinking in the United States when the federal and state constitutions were crafted. It was also part of the early legal landscape in North Carolina, enabling local governments to facilitate construction of necessary public improvements. Beginning with piecemeal legislative authorization of the use of eminent domain for particular projects, the laws governing local government use of eminent domain have evolved into a comprehensive statutory mechanism applicable for most common public functions. Nonetheless, the law remains complex and its application is not always straightforward.

1.2.1 Eminent Domain in the Republic

The revolutionary founders apparently did not question the government's eminent domain power despite its potential for abuse. As one legal scholar noted, "[T]here seems no indication that the Revolutionary experience itself had created any particular alarm about the expropriation power. Examination of the Declaration of Independence and of ten other important Revolutionary documents revealed that, while the British were scoundrels in a thousand ways, they never abused eminent domain."[5] The persistence of eminent domain can be reconciled with American libertarian principles, as reflected in the philosophy of John Locke, whose ideas Thomas Jefferson expounded in the Declaration. As Locke said in "An Essay Concerning Civil Government," a right to own private property is essential to happiness: "[T]he supreme power cannot take from any man any part of his property without his own

---

4. Grotius, De Jure Belli et Pacis, Lib. 3, c. 20, *quoted in* Wissler v. Yadkin River Power Co., 158 N.C. 465, 466, 74 S.E. 460, 460 (1912).

5. William B. Stoebuck, *A General Theory of Eminent Domain*, 47 WASH. L. REV. 553, 594 (1972).

consent. For the preservation of property being the end of government, and that for which men enter into society, it necessarily supposes and requires, that the people should have property."[6] Locke also said that this right carried with it some responsibilities: "It is true governments cannot be supported without great charge, and it is fit every one who enjoys his share of the protection should pay out of his estate his proportion for the maintenance of it. But still it must be with his own consent, *i.e.* the consent of the majority, giving it either by themselves, or their representatives chosen by them."[7] As Locke explained it, private ownership is part of a compact in which owners are deemed to have consented to a fair contribution to the common good, as determined by elected representatives.

The notion that eminent domain is part of a compact between a citizen and the representative government explains why the power lies with the elected legislature and may only be used by governments when the legislature has authorized such use. Federal and state constitutions affirm the individual's right to expect that governments will employ this power only according to laws duly enacted by the legislatures.[8] This protection appears in the North Carolina Constitution in Article I, Section 19, which provides as follows: "No person shall be taken, imprisoned, or disseized of his freehold, liberties, or privileges, or outlawed, or exiled, or in any manner deprived of his life, liberty, or property, but by the law of the land." While the eminent domain power is implicit rather than explicit, the requirement to act according to "the law of the land" when property is taken is clearly stated.

1.2.2 Evolution of Eminent Domain Law in North Carolina

The owner's constitutional guaranty against losing private property for public use without compensation was expressed in a jurisprudential environment in which the legitimacy of eminent domain was not questioned. Eighteenth century English and colonial laws, which are the foundation of the American legal system, authorized land condemnation for roads, bridges, fortifications, and other improvements.[9] For example, a 1764 colonial act in North Caro-

---

6. JOHN LOCKE, TWO TREATISES OF GOVERNMENT 165 (McMaster University ed., 2005); *see* Stoebuck, *supra* note 5, at 566–67 (explaining the application of Locke's philosophy to eminent domain).

7. LOCKE, *supra* note 6, at 166.

8. Stoebuck, *supra* note 5, at 567, 586.

9. *Id.* at 561–62.

lina empowered county courts to lay out public roads, establish ferries, and build bridges "for the Use and Ease of the Inhabitants of this Province."[10] The North Carolina Supreme Court never cast doubt about the state government's power of eminent domain. The court's view was expressed in an 1837 case as follows:

> The right of the public to private property, to the extent that the use of it is needful and advantageous to the public, must, we think, be universally acknowledged. Writers upon the laws of nature and nations treat it as a right inherent in society. . . . But practically, it is immaterial whether the right be supposed to have been impliedly reserved because it ought not to be granted, or because it is a portion of the national sovereignty which is inalienable by the government, or whether the right is created by the public necessity, which at the time calls for its exercise,—its existence in every state is indispensable and incontestable.[11]

In this and other judicial opinions, the jurists have reflected acceptance of eminent domain as an inherent governmental power, which lies dormant until the elected legislature authorizes an arm of government to exercise it.[12]

In North Carolina, therefore, the state power of eminent domain rests with the General Assembly. Whenever a local government exercises eminent domain, it does so through the delegated authority of the elected state representatives.[13] The state-based source of eminent domain power is illustrated by a North Carolina local government's power to take property in another local government's jurisdiction[14]—under certain conditions a local government is authorized to exercise state power, not any power inherent in local government itself.

---

10. Laws of N.C., ch. 3 (1764) *in* 1 THE FIRST LAWS OF THE STATE OF NORTH CAROLINA 212 (1984).

11. Raleigh & Gaston R.R. v. Davis, 19 N.C. 451, 455–56 (1837).

12. 1A JULIUS L. SACKMAN, NICHOLS ON EMINENT DOMAIN §§ 3.03[1], 3.03[3][a] (3d ed. 2007).

13. Hunter v. City of Pittsburgh, 207 U.S. 161, 178–79 (1907).

14. N.C. GEN. STAT. ANN. § 40A-3(b) (2007) (hereinafter G.S.), which authorizes local governments to exercise eminent domain for the common local government functions, states that the power applies to projects "either inside or outside" the local government's boundaries. The statutes contain some restrictions on this extraterritorial power. *See* Section 1.11 below.

North Carolina state government has always delegated eminent domain powers to local governments for local public projects, and local governments have used them routinely to deliver essential infrastructure. For example, a 1784 law empowered counties to construct roads in routes "laid out by a jury of freeholders to the greatest advantage of the inhabitants, and as little as may be to the prejudice of inclosures which lay out; and such damages as private persons may sustain shall be done and ascertained by the same jury on oath . . . and all damages hereafter to be thus assessed shall be deemed a county charge, and be defrayed from the tax on each county laid for contingent charges."[15] This requirement that compensation be paid only for "inclosed" land reflects the prevailing view at that time that new roads benefited open, or unimproved, land, and an owner should not be compensated when property is enhanced.[16] What might surprise many today is that the state legislature also authorized counties and cities to conscript those living near the new road to work on its construction, for up to six days annually for those who lived east of the Blue Ridge, and ten days for those who lived west of it.[17]

Throughout the nineteenth century, as the state developed and land was needed for highways, canals, and railroads, the General Assembly passed local acts to authorize use of eminent domain by local governments and public carriers. Such acts typically would authorize acquisition of a particular stretch of land for a project and direct commissioners to summon a jury to determine the "damages" to be paid to the owner.[18] The first statute establishing a more general procedure for repeated use was enacted in 1871, for use by railroads.[19] The statute prescribed a procedure for appointment of three commissioners of appraisal in the county superior courts. The commissioners, who were required to be "disinterested and competent freeholders," were directed to determine "the compensation to be made to the owners or persons interested in the real estate proposed to be taken."[20] Other legislation delegated eminent domain power for other public purposes, such as an act granting county boards of education the power to take up to one acre for a school by paying "the cash

---

15. Laws of N.C., ch. 14, II, sec. 3 (1784) *in* THE FIRST LAWS OF THE STATE OF NORTH CAROLINA 532 (1984).

16. Stoebuck, *supra* note 5, at 582–83.

17. 1879 N.C. Sess. Laws ch. 82, sec. 4; 1880 N.C. Sess. Laws ch. 30, sec. 2.

18. 1870–71 N.C. Sess. Laws ch. 148 (for a public road from Sparta, North Carolina, to the Virginia line).

19. 1871–72 N.C. Sess. Laws ch. 138, secs. 13–22.

20. *Id.*

value thereof" to the owner, in an amount determined by "three disinterested citizens," with a right of appeal to the superior court.[21] In 1917 the General Assembly generally authorized cities to take land for streets, utilities, recreational areas, sewage facilities, and other traditionally public uses by the same procedure that had been created for railroads in 1871.[22] The counties' statutory authority for eminent domain was reorganized in 1973, and counties were authorized to use the same procedure provided for cities and towns and originally authorized for railroads.[23]

This summary of the history of eminent domain statutes in North Carolina shows that eminent domain law was mostly enacted piecemeal. By the 1970s the North Carolina statutes included over eighteen separate procedures for eminent domain acquisitions.[24] As one commentator said at the time, "Much of this law, some of which predates the Revolutionary War, [was] antiquated and unused."[25] The most significant reorganization and unification of the state's local government eminent domain laws occurred in 1981, with enactment of a statutory structure in Chapter 40A that remains in effect today. The legislative purpose of this consolidation was declared as follows: "It is the intent of the General Assembly that the procedures provided by this Chapter shall be the exclusive condemnation procedures to be used in this State by all private condemnors and all local public condemnors."[26] Chapter 40A lists the most common uses or benefits for which local governments might exercise eminent domain powers and provides a standard procedure for superior court actions, which are discussed in detail in Chapter 2, to employ the power. Chapter 40A also provides guidance for awarding compensation for property taken by local governments, including the process for determining compensation amounts, which is discussed in Chapter 3.

Despite the consolidation and clarification that the General Assembly accomplished with enactment of Chapter 40A, the scope of eminent domain powers and the applicable procedures are not all encompassed within that chapter. Some public authorities are identified in Chapter 40A as having

---

21. 1881 N.C. Sess. Laws ch. 200, sec. 55.

22. 1917 N.C. Sess. Laws ch. 136, sub. chs. IV, VII.

23. 1973 N.C. Sess. Laws ch. 822, sec. 1, art. 8.

24. Robert E. Phay, *The Eminent Domain Procedure of North Carolina: The Need for Legislative Action*, 45 N.C. L. Rev. 587, 588 (1967).

25. *Id.* at 587–88.

26. 1981 N.C. Sess. Laws ch. 919, sec. 1.

eminent domain powers, but the scope of their powers and the required procedures are set forth in other statutes. Yet other authorizations for eminent
domain can still be found in other statutes and local acts. Consequently, any
local government considering use of eminent domain must research the various possible sources of such power to determine whether the power exists,
the nature of any constraints on its exercise, the procedures that must be
followed, and the compensation that must be paid to any owners.

1.3   Public Use and Benefit

The Fifth Amendment to the United States Constitution prohibits private
property from being "taken *for public use* without just compensation."[27] The
North Carolina Constitution does not mention eminent domain or "public
use." It states that "[n]o person shall be taken, imprisoned, or disseized of
his freehold, liberties, or privileges, or outlawed, or exiled, or in any manner deprived of his life, liberty, or property, but by the law of the land."[28]
The courts therefore have only very general language in the constitutions on
which to base their decisions about the permissible extent of compelled government acquisitions. The courts generally have deferred to the legislatures
for determinations about when the use of eminent domain is sufficiently tied
to a public need to satisfy the public use requirement explicitly stated in the
federal Constitution and implicit in the North Carolina constitution.

1.3.1   United States Supreme Court on Permissible
Eminent Domain

The United States Supreme Court summarized its approach as follows: "The
role of the judiciary in determining whether [the power of eminent domain] is
being exercised for a public purpose is an extremely narrow one,"[29] and that a
taking is for "public use" as described in the Fifth Amendment of the United
States Constitution if it helps to achieve a "public purpose."[30] That is, the land
taken by eminent domain need not be actually *used* by the public.[31] Recently,

---

27. U.S. Const. amend. V (emphasis added).
28. N.C. Const. art. I, § 19.
29. Berman v. Parker, 348 U.S. 26, 32 (1954).
30. *Id.* at 32–36.
31. *Id.*; Fallbrook Irrigation Dist. v. Bradley, 164 U.S. 112, 158–64 (1896).

in *Kelo v. City of New London*,[32] a case that received a great deal of public attention and spurred much legislative activity, the Supreme Court held that the Fifth Amendment was not violated when the eminent domain power was used to acquire land through a government's appointed development agent for conveyance to a private party.[33] The land was to be included in an integrated plan developed by the government to rejuvenate an economically troubled area.[34] This decision reflected the Court's deferential approach to reviewing legislative acts authorizing eminent domain, which it had previously described as follows: "Subject to specific constitutional limitations, when the legislature has spoken, the public interest has been declared in terms well-nigh conclusive. In such cases the legislature, not the judiciary, is the main guardian of the public needs to be served by social legislation, whether it be Congress legislating concerning the District of Columbia or the States legislating concerning local affairs."[35] The Supreme Court also noted that it has "eschewed rigid formulas and intrusive scrutiny in favor of affording legislatures broad latitude in determining what public needs justify the use of the takings power."[36]

In *Kelo* and in other opinions, the United States Supreme Court has made clear that state legislatures not only have broad discretion to designate public purposes for the exercise of eminent domain, but also that representative assemblies could decline to invoke this power or restrict its application as narrowly as they wished. The Court expressly noted in *Kelo* that "nothing in our opinion precludes any State from placing further restrictions on its exercise of the takings power. Indeed, many States already impose 'public use' requirements that are stricter than the federal baseline."[37]

1.3.2 North Carolina Law on Permissible Eminent Domain

Consistent with the approach followed by the United States Supreme Court, the North Carolina Supreme Court has also restrained its role in assessing the scope of the eminent domain power under state law. The state supreme court stated the following about the North Carolina Constitution: "As we have stated on numerous occasions, the statutory phrase 'the public use or benefit' is incapable of a precise definition applicable to all situations. Rather,

---

32. 545 U.S. 469 (2005).
33. *Id.* at 483–90.
34. *Id.* at 473–75, 478.
35. Berman v. Parker, 348 U.S. 26, 32 (1954) (citations omitted).
36. *Kelo*, 545 U.S. at 483.
37. *Id.* at 489.

because of the progressive demands of an ever-changing society and the perpetually fluid concept of governmental duty and function, the phrase is elastic and keeps pace with changing times."[38] The court has also noted this state's legislature's discretion to withhold eminent domain power: "Any state legislature, and therefore the North Carolina General Assembly, has the right to determine what portion of this power it will delegate to public or private corporations to be used for the public's benefit."[39]

The North Carolina Supreme Court has been explicitly deferential to the state legislature's delegation of eminent domain power. As the court said, "Under our division of governmental power into three branches—executive, legislative, and judicial—only the legislative can authorize the exercise of the power of eminent domain and prescribe the manner of its use. The right of eminent domain lies dormant in the State until the legislature, by statute, confers the power and points out the occasion, mode, conditions and agencies for its exercise."[40] The court has scrutinized whether particular uses of delegated power exceed what is constitutionally permissible and has used several tests in doing so. It has held that a proposed use is permissible if it satisfies a "public use test," which is met if "the general public has a right to a definite use of the property sought to be condemned."[41] This use requirement is met if the public has the right to use the land; actual use is not required.[42] Consequently, a road ending in a cul de sac was held to be for public use even though only a few property owners were likely to make regular use of it.[43] In another case, the court held that an air cargo facility was for a public purpose even if the facility would be used primarily by one carrier, based on the following conclusion: "The arrangement advances the primary goal of giving effect to the people's general desire for better seaports and airports. As such, the greater benefits flow to the people, as they have constitutionally directed, with their understanding that there will be incidental benefits to private companies involved."[44]

---

38. Carolina Tel. & Tel. Co. v. McLeod, 321 N.C. 426, 429–30, 364 S.E.2d 399, 401 (1988) (citations omitted).

39. *Id.* at 429, 364 S.E.2d at 401.

40. State v. Core Banks Club Properties Inc., 275 N.C. 328, 334, 167 S.E.2d 385, 389 (1969).

41. *McLeod*, 321 N.C. at 430, 364 S.E.2d at 401.

42. *Id.* at 430–31, 364 S.E.2d at 401.

43. *Id.* at 430, 364 S.E.2d at 401.

44. Piedmont Triad Airport Auth. v. Urbine, 354 N.C. 336, 343, 554 S.E.2d 331, 335 (2001).

The North Carolina Supreme Court has held that eminent domain may be used to acquire property that the public will not functionally "use" without offending the state constitution if the purpose satisfies a "public benefit test," which the court defines as follows:

> Generally, under the public benefit test, a given condemnor's desired use of the condemned property in question is for "the public use or benefit" if that use would contribute to the general welfare and prosperity of the public at large. However, judicial decisions in this and other states reveal that not just any benefit to the general public will suffice under this test. Rather, the taking must "furnish the public with some necessity or convenience which cannot readily be furnished without the aid of some governmental power, and which is required by the public as such."[45]

The courts have held that an acquisition by eminent domain can be considered for a public use or benefit even if only one person directly benefits if the acquisition will be part of the extension of a public utility or improvement. In *Carolina Telephone & Telegraph Co. v. McLeod*[46] the North Carolina Supreme Court, affirming the constitutionality of using eminent domain to extend telephone service to a single customer, said, "The exercise of eminent domain for a public purpose which is primary and paramount will not be defeated by the fact that incidentally a private use or benefit will result which will not of itself warrant the exercise of a power. . . . The controlling question is whether the paramount reason for the taking of the land to which objection is made is the public interest, to which benefits to private interests are merely incidental, or whether, on the other hand, the private interests are paramount and controlling and the public interests merely incidental."[47] Therefore, when the proposed use has both public and private traits, the court determines the taking to be for a constitutionally permissible public use "so long as the private use in question is incidental to

---

45. Carolina Tel. & Tel. Co. v. McLeod, 321 N.C. 426, 432, 364 S.E.2d 399, 402 (1988) (quoting Charlotte v. Heath, 226 N.C. 750, 755, 40 S.E.2d 600, 604 (1946) (quoting 18 AM. JUR. *Eminent Domain* § 38 (1938))).

46. 321 N.C. 426, 364 S.E.2d 399 (1988).

47. *Id.* at 433, 364 S.E.2d at 403 (quoting Highway Comm'n v. School, 276 N.C. 556, 562–63, 173 S.E.2d 909, 914 (1970) (quoting 26 AM. JUR. 2d *Eminent Domain* §§ 32, 33 (1966))).

the paramount public use."[48] This is also true, for example, when property acquired for a school also provided a private owner public road access.[49] There was also no violation of the public use requirement when a particular citizen gained utility access as a result of an acquisition to extend a transmission line, because, the court reasoned, telephone service is a public necessity and the utility could use eminent domain to make service widely available.[50] Similarly, the extension of a sewer system in connection with a municipal annexation, which more particularly benefited the annexed area but was part of the community's growth and development, was also held to be for public use and benefit.[51] A statutorily authorized use of eminent domain that probably has the least clear connection to public use or benefit allows a private individual or entity to acquire an easement over another's land for a cart way, church road, or mill road. The North Carolina Supreme Court has held that this use of eminent domain is sufficiently "quasi-public,"[52] though in a recent case a judge expressed the opinion that the power was being used for an inappropriately private purpose.[53]

In a few cases, the North Carolina Supreme Court has held that eminent domain was being used inappropriately for a private purpose. In 1920 the North Carolina Supreme Court held that a railroad company authorized to use eminent domain to build a railroad could not use that power to acquire land to build a logging road for its private logging business.[54] The court also held that the state highway commission could not properly use eminent domain to take land to build a dead-end access road from a public highway to properties owned by members of a family at the family's request.[55] The court said that "any use by, or any benefit for, the general public will be only incidental and purely conjectural; that it is not for a public use, and that no public necessity, convenience, or utility exists for the State Highway Commission to condemn" the land for the private access road.[56]

---

48. *McLeod,* 321 N.C. at 433, 364 S.E.2d at 403.

49. *Id.* at 433–34, 364 S.E.2d at 403–4.

50. *Id.* at 434, 364 S.E.2d at 403–4.

51. Tucker v. City of Kannapolis, 159 N.C. App. 174, 582 S.E.2d 697 (2003).

52. Barber v. Griffin, 158 N.C. 348, 350, 74 S.E. 110, 111 (1912).

53. Jones v. Winckelmann, 134 N.C. App. 143, 146, 516 S.E.2d 876, 878 (1999) (Lewis, J., concurring).

54. Bradshaw v. Hilton Lumber Co., 179 N.C. 501, 103 S.E. 69 (1920).

55. State Highway Comm'n v. Batts, 265 N.C. 346, 144 S.E.2d 126 (1965).

56. *Id.* at 360, 144 S.E.2d at 136.

The court later distinguished the characteristics of the project, described as being undertaken on behalf of the owners who requested the road be built, from those of the use of eminent domain to build an access road that would be "an incidental part of a comprehensive and complex highway project."[57]

The North Carolina Supreme Court has also regularly upheld the legislature's discretion to delegate the eminent domain power to a nongovernmental entity charged with a function deemed to be a public use or benefit. North Carolina was among the many states that in the nineteenth century authorized mill owners to use state eminent domain powers to acquire flowage easements from other landowners,[58] and the state's supreme court analogized such powers to those properly entrusted to municipal and county governments for public purposes. Courts throughout the United States quickly endorsed the ability of state legislatures to delegate eminent domain powers to railroads and other companies understood to offer public facilities or utilities. As explained in an early New York opinion that many state courts found persuasive, "[R]ailroads, for the conveyance of travelers, or the transportation of merchandise from one part of the State to another were public improvements and for the public benefit. . . . The right itself might be exercised by the government through its immediate officers or agents, or indirectly through the medium of corporate bodies or private individuals."[59] The same principles apply to other public utilities, and the notion of what constitutes a public utility has evolved with industrialization and urban development. For example, in 1912 the North Carolina Supreme Court held that the eminent domain power could be delegated to electric companies. The court said, "This power of eminent domain is conferred upon corporations affected with public use, not so much for the benefit of the corporations themselves, but for the use and benefit of the people at large. What are *public utilities* has been pretty well settled by the courts, but with the advance of science and the arts the scope of such utilities must necessarily be constantly increased."[60] The legislature has since delegated eminent domain

---

57. North Carolina State Highway Comm'n v. Asheville School Inc., 276 N.C. 556, 562, 173 S.E.2d 909, 914 (1970).

58. 1868–69 N.C. Sess. Laws ch. 158.

59. Bloodgood v. Mohawk & Hudson R.R., 18 Wend. 9, 13–14 (N.Y. Sup. Ct. 1837).

60. Wissler v. Yadkin River Power Co., 158 N.C. 465, 466–67, 74 S.E. 460, 460 (1912) (emphasis in original).

powers to a wide variety of utilities, carriers, institutions, and agencies given power under legislative acts to provide public services.[61]

Notwithstanding the broad discretion the courts have afforded the legislatures to determine appropriate uses of the eminent domain power, the North Carolina Supreme Court has made clear that courts have a duty to strike down takings that are not for public use or benefit.[62] The use of eminent domain for economic development has tested the limits of the North Carolina courts' deference to the state legislature, as in other jurisdictions. In *Redevelopment Commission of Greensboro v. Security National Bank of Greensboro*,[63] the North Carolina Supreme Court upheld the constitutionality of an urban redevelopment law allowing a municipal redevelopment commission to take property in a "blighted area," defined as an area in which there is a predominance of dilapidated buildings or unsanitary and unsafe conditions.[64] This was consistent with an earlier holding that a state is performing a public function when it clears slums.[65] In two cases decided in the late 1960s and early 1970s, the North Carolina Supreme Court cast doubt on use of government powers for redevelopment. In *Mitchell v. North Carolina Industrial Development Financing Authority*,[66] the court held that the state could not appropriate funds to an industrial development authority to acquire sites and construct and equip them for purely private ownership because this was "not for a public use or purpose."[67] In *Foster v. North Carolina Medical Care Commission*,[68] the North Carolina Supreme Court held that the finance and construction of hospital facilities to be privately owned and operated after public bonds were retired

---

61. *See* G.S. 40A-3(a) (private condemnors); G.S. 40A-3(b) (local public condemnors); G.S. 40A-3(c) (public agencies, boards, and other authorities).

62. *E.g.,* Stout v. City of Durham, 121 N.C. App. 716, 718, 468 S.E.2d 254, 257 (1996) (reviewing public use or benefit); Cobb v. Atlantic Coast Line R.R., 172 N.C. 58, 61, 89 S.E. 807, 808 (1916) (describing judicial review of public use or benefit); Stratford v. City of Greensboro, 124 N.C. 127, 132–33, 32 S.E. 394, 396 (1899) (reviewing whether public or private use).

63. 252 N.C. 595, 114 S.E.2d 688 (1960).

64. *Id.* at 606–11, 114 S.E.2d at 695–98.

65. Wells v. Housing Auth., 213 N.C. 744, 197 S.E. 693 (1938), *overruled by* N.C. CONST. art. V, § 14.

66. 273 N.C. 137, 159 S.E.2d 745 (1968).

67. *Id.* at 159, 159 S.E.2d at 761.

68. 283 N.C. 110, 195 S.E.2d 517 (1973).

were "not . . . expenditure[s] for a public purpose."[69] The court distinguished its cases in which it upheld use of eminent domain for redevelopment on the ground that "the primary purpose of the [redevelopment] legislation was to protect the public health by eliminating existing slums, replacing them with safe and sanitary housing or other buildings and assuring that the blighted condition would not return. The fact that such project would benefit individuals permitted to rent the new housing units or other new buildings or to purchase, own and use them, after the accomplishment of the primary purpose of the law, was deemed incidental thereto."[70] In the case of bonds for privately owned hospitals, however, the court said that "the Act has no purpose separate and apart from the operation by and ultimate conveyance of the hospital facility to the lessee thereof."[71] However, in 1996 the court departed from its previous scrutiny in cases involving economic development in *Maready v. City of Winston-Salem*.[72] The court held that incentive grants offered to encourage private industry to relocate had a constitutionally sufficient public purpose in "alleviat[ing] conditions of unemployment and fiscal distress and . . . increas[ing] the local tax base."[73] The court said that notions about permissible public purposes had to evolve with changes in land use conditions and the need for economic development.[74] In 2003 the North Carolina Constitution was amended to give the General Assembly the power to grant to local governments and other public authorities the power to "finance public improvements associated with private development projects," provided certain methods for allocating tax assessments to project financing are followed.[75]

This summary demonstrates that the courts' analysis of permissible uses of eminent domain has changed over time. Most recently, state courts have

---

69. Although *Foster* was not an eminent domain case, the court said that the analysis of public purposes "is employed in the same sense." *Id.* at 126–27, 195 S.E.2d at 528. In a later case, the court made a distinction between the term "public purpose" as allowed for tax expenditures and "public use" as appropriate for eminent domain but said "the analysis in determining both is often similar." Piedmont Triad Airport Auth. v. Urbine, 354 N.C. 336, 339, 554 S.E.2d 331, 332 (2001).

70. *Foster*, 283 N.C. at 126–27, 195 S.E.2d at 528.

71. *Id.*

72. 342 N.C. 708, 467 S.E.2d 615 (1996).

73. *Id.* at 727, 467 S.E.2d at 627.

74. *Id.*

75. N.C. CONST. art. V, § 14.

reflected the approach taken by the United States Supreme Court, generally deferring to legislative determinations about what constitutes public use and benefit in light of modern conditions and perceived needs for government action to address public interests. Local governments considering use of eminent domain for purposes that are not clearly for a traditional public use must be attuned to the courts' most recent opinions.

1.3.3 Review of Extent of Legislative Authorization

The cases discussed above involved challenges to legislative delegation of eminent domain power. The courts have not been favorably disposed to attempted use of eminent domain when the legislature had not expressly granted such power to a local government or other authority undertaking a public project or service. The North Carolina Supreme Court noted, "'The exercise of the power being against common right, it cannot be implied or inferred from vague or doubtful language, but must be given in express terms or by necessary implication. If the act is silent on the subject, and the powers given by it can be exercised without resort to condemnation, it is presumed that the Legislature intended that the necessary property should be acquired by contract.'"[76] The court held that the power will not be deemed to have been implied unless the legislature's intent to do so is inescapable; as the court said, the need to use eminent domain "must not be a necessity created by the company itself for its own convenience or for the sake of economy."[77]

The North Carolina Supreme Court has insisted that a local government or government entity may not assume it has eminent domain powers merely because it is authorized to engage in activities for which such power could be appropriate. The legislature must express its intent to authorize use of eminent domain. For example, in *State v. Core Banks Club Properties Inc.*,[78] the North Carolina Supreme Court held that although the General Assembly may authorize

---

76. Commissioners of Beaufort County v. Bonner, 153 N.C. 66, 69, 68 S.E. 970, 972 (1910) (quoting 1 JOHN LEWIS, EMINENT DOMAIN § 240); *see also* Eppley v. Bryson City, 157 N.C. 487, 488, 73 S.E. 197, 197–98 (1911) ("[I]n order that a municipal corporation shall lawfully exercise the right of eminent domain the power must be expressly conferred or arise by necessary implication, and the procedure necessary to give it effect must be provided"); *Bonner,* 153 N.C. at 69–70, 68 S.E. at 972 (same).

77. *Bonner,* 153 N.C. at 70, 68 S.E. at 972.

78. 275 N.C. 328, 167 S.E.2d 385 (1969).

a county to use eminent domain to acquire land for recreational purposes, the power must be given expressly or by necessary implication. The court held that a General Assembly resolution endorsing a national seashore project and directing state agencies to assist was an insufficient basis for use of eminent domain.[79] In another case the court held that a county did not have eminent domain power to acquire a public landing when the statute gave the commissioners the power to establish public landings but did not mention eminent domain.[80] The court has held that a government authority seeking to acquire land already in public use must have very clearly been granted eminent domain power.[81]

1.4   Owner's Right to Compensation

The United States Constitution expressly requires that "just compensation" must be paid to an owner whose property is taken by the government through eminent domain. The Fourteenth Amendment to the United States Constitution guarantees the right to just compensation when property is taken by a state for public use by providing that "[n]o State shall . . . deprive any person of . . . property, without due process of law."[82] The government's right to acquire property is deemed implicit, and, as the United States Supreme Court has said, the rights of "property owners are satisfied when they receive that just compensation which the Fifth Amendment exacts as the price of the taking."[83] The amount of the compensation must be determined by due process. As the Court explained, "Due process of law as applied to judicial proceedings instituted for the taking of private property for public use means, therefore, such process as recognizes the right of the owner to be compensated if his property be wrested from him and transferred to the public."[84] State

---

79. *Id.* at 331–37, 167 S.E.2d at 386–91.

80. *Bonner*, 153 N.C. at 70, 68 S.E. at 972.

81. Southern Ry. Co. v. City of Greensboro, 247 N.C. 321, 101 S.E.2d 347 (1957).

82. U.S. Const. amend. XIV, sec. 1.

83. Berman v. Parker, 348 U.S. 26, 36 (1954).

84. Chicago B. & Q. R.R. v. City of Chicago, 166 U.S. 226, 236 (1897); *see also* Long v. City of Charlotte, 306 N.C. 187, 196, 293 S.E. 2d 101, 107–08 (1982) (Fourteenth Amendment Due Process Clause prohibits a state from taking property without just compensation).

courts uniformly have reiterated that a private property owner has a right to be paid just compensation for property taken by the government.[85]

Among the state constitutions, only North Carolina's does not expressly state that the government must pay for any private property it takes.[86] The North Carolina Supreme Court does not view this silence as an indication that just compensation is not constitutionally required. The court considers the principle to be embedded in the constitutional prohibition against depriving any person of "life, liberty, or property, but by the law of the land."[87] In an 1856 case, the court eloquently described the principle as follows:

> Whether private property can be taken for public use without compensation, is a question that we are not called on to decide. There is no clause of our Constitution, or Bill of Rights, which expressly requires it. But the justice of making compensation is so obvious, that the omission of a clause requiring it, can only be accounted for upon the supposition, that it was taken for granted, that no act of such gross oppression would ever be perpetrated by the representatives of a free people. The laws of Athens prescribed no punishment for parricide, for it was taken for granted that no one would ever be guilty of a crime so horrid.[88]

Accordingly, the court has held that "the law of the land" means with payment of just compensation as a matter of principle, just as the United States Constitution requires. As the court explained, "We recognize the fundamental right to just compensation as so grounded in natural law and justice that it is part of the fundamental law of this State, and imposes upon a governmental agency taking private property for public use a correlative duty to make just compensation to the owner of the property taken. This principle is considered in North Carolina as an integral part of 'the law of the land' within the meaning of Article I, Section 19 of our State Constitution."[89]

---

85. 1 Julius L. Sackman, Nichols on Eminent Domain § 1.3 (3d ed. 2007).

86. *Id.*

87. N.C. Const. art. I, § 19.

88. Freedle v. North Carolina Rail Co., 49 N.C. 89, 90 (1856).

89. *Long*, 306 N.C. at 196, 293 S.E. 2d at 107–08; *see also* State v. Core Banks Club Properties Inc., 275 N.C. 328, 334, 167 S.E.2d 385, 388 (1969) ("The right to take private property for public use, the power of eminent domain, is one of the prerogatives of a sovereign state. The right is inherent in sovereignty; it is not conferred

The extent of the compensation considered to be just is discussed in Chapter 3.

1.5   Rights Subject to Eminent Domain

The government's dormant power of eminent domain extends to all nature of property, whether real estate, personal property, contract rights, or other property interests. The authority given local condemnors under Chapter 40A extends only to all forms of real property. The statute defines property that can be acquired by eminent domain as "any right, title, or interest in land, including leases and options to buy or sell. 'Property' also includes rights of access, rights-of-way, easements, water rights, air rights, and any other privilege or appurtenance in or to the possession, use, and enjoyment of land."[90]

The two most common types of property interests acquired by local governments are fee interests and easement rights. A fee interest is full ownership with the right to use, encumber, and convey the real estate. Fee interests are delineated with boundaries described by distances and courses, references to natural or human-installed monuments, or by reference to depictions on plans. An area is defined as a single tract or parcel based on how owners have acquired and conveyed the property. A single owner can own multiple adjoining tracts and acquire and convey them in a single deed or in separate deeds for each tract. As described in sections 2.6 and 3.6 below, defining the relationship of the land being acquired to the land from which it is subdivided or to other parcels in the same chain of title can be important in determining necessary parties to an eminent domain proceeding and the amount of required compensation. The chain of conveyances for the subject tract and all plans on which the conveyances relied must be examined in order to understand the full extent of ownership rights and encumbrances. Accordingly, condemnors should consider conducting or engaging a title search in connection with offers to acquire real property and before commencing eminent domain proceedings.

An easement interest is a right to limited use of another's land. A typical kind of easement is a right to cross another's land for a driveway or a

---

by constitutions. Its exercise, however, is limited by the constitutional requirements of due process and payment of just compensation for property condemned").

90. G.S. 40A-2(7).

utility's right to cross property with power lines that serve the property or other utility users. Condemnors may acquire temporary easement rights to store equipment and materials or to cross property during construction of public improvements.[91] Easements also can include a wide variety of other kinds of rights in another's land, such as the right to a view that requires an owner to restrict vegetation and construction.[92] The nature and extent of any easement right and any restrictions or obligations that accompany that right are defined by the instruments in the chain of title, complemented by interpretative case law that supplies reasonable terms when none are specified. Easements often are described in deeds when an owner subdivides but can also be specified in separate recorded instruments such as a declaration of covenants. Easement rights also can be acquired through implication, necessity, and prescriptive use over a long period of time; such rights are not legally certain unless they are set by agreement or adjudged by a court. The complexity of easement law and the high potential for disagreement about easement rights warrant special care when condemnors are acquiring easements or property subject to easements. When easement rights are acquired, condemnors will want to define those rights clearly and fully in the eminent domain proceeding and in the judgment and plat that will thereafter define title.

Real estate involves many other complex and evolving legal issues that could arise in an eminent domain action. Two cases concerning restrictive covenants demonstrate the potential conceptual difficulties involving the confluence of government activities and owners' reasonable expectations about real estate rights. In *City of Raleigh v. Edwards*[93] the North Carolina Supreme Court considered a landowner's claim in response to a municipal acquisition of a parcel in a neighborhood subject to covenants restricting property to residential use. The city violated the covenants by installing a water tank. The court noted that restrictive covenants can be a valuable property right for those who benefit from them. The court explained that such a covenant,

---

91. *E.g.,* Colonial Pipeline Co. v. Weaver, 310 N.C. 93, 107, 310 S.E.2d 338, 346 (1984) (discussing valuation of temporary construction easement); City of Winston-Salem v. Ferrell, 79 N.C. App. 103, 111–13, 338 S.E.2d 794, 800–801 (1986) (inverse condemnation of temporary construction easement).

92. Greensboro–High Point Airport Auth. v. Irvin, 2 N.C. App. 341, 163 S.E.2d 118 (1968).

93. 235 N.C. 671, 71 S.E.2d 396 (1952).

being in the nature of an equitable servitude, is an interest in land and must be paid for when taken. The theory is that these restrictions impose negative easements on the land restricted in favor of and appendant to the rest of the land in the restricted area, and when a particular parcel thereof is appropriated for a public use that will violate the restrictions, such appropriation amounts in a constitutional sense to a taking or damaging of property of the other landowners for whose benefit the restrictions are imposed.[94]

In *Carolina Mills Inc. v. Catawba County Board of Education*[95] the court of appeals followed this same reasoning, refusing to issue an injunction to prevent a board of education from installing school tennis courts in an area restricted to residential use, holding that the landowner's remedy was damages for the diminution in value resulting from loss of the covenant's beneficial effects.[96]

Although Chapter 40A is concerned with use of eminent domain to acquire real property, the General Assembly could by legislation constitutionally authorize local governments to acquire other types of property interests. As discussed in Chapter 4, the courts have recognized that when government takes other kinds of property, it must compensate the owner regardless of whether the government had legislative authorization to take the property. Most such cases involve occupation of real estate. However, the law constrains government's ability to take other types of property, as might occur, for example, when contributions are required in exchange for development approval[97] or a franchise right is terminated in connection with changes in a public service.[98] Chapter 4 explains the nature of owners' claims in connection with various types of property interests.

---

94. *Id.* at 677, 71 S.E.2d at 401.

95. 27 N.C. App. 524, 219 S.E.2d 509 (1975).

96. *Id.* at 527, 219 S.E.2d at 511–12.

97. *E.g.,* River Birch Associates v. City of Raleigh, 326 N.C. 100, 388 S.E.2d 538 (1990) (compelling conveyance in exchange for development approval).

98. *E.g.,* Stillings v. City of Winston-Salem, 311 N.C. 689, 319 S.E.2d 233 (1984) (solid waste collection franchise agreement terminated).

1.6 Authority to Determine Property Needed

North Carolina local governments have discretion to determine the property to be taken, provided the use to which it will be applied is legislatively authorized and constitutionally permissible. Decisions about project needs are not subject to judicial inquiry except when facts indicate the condemnor is acting in bad faith or oppressively or there is a manifest abuse of discretion.[99] The courts recognize that governments must be afforded discretion to make decisions about property to be acquired to implement public projects. As the North Carolina Supreme Court noted:

> [T]he economic feasibility of the proposed use is for the legislative or administrative body to determine. With that determination the courts may not interfere, except upon a clear showing of abuse of discretion such as to make the taking of the property an arbitrary and capricious interference with the right of the owner thereto. Thus, in the absence of a showing of bad faith, . . . the courts will not interfere with the legislative or administrative determination that the taking of the particular property is necessary for the successful operation of the proposed project or prevent the taking on the ground that another site would be better, cheaper or otherwise preferable.[100]

As the North Carolina Court of Appeals explained, "Even where less intrusive means of accomplishing the public purpose exist, a condemnation will not be invalidated when the taking is not arbitrary and capricious and is necessary to accomplish the purpose."[101] A condemnor acquiring property for an authorized purpose has the discretion to determine the scope and location of the project. For example, the courts will not scrutinize a decision to widen a street without a showing of bad faith or obvious abuse of discretion.[102] A condemnor's discretion also includes the determination of the extent of the

---

99. City of Charlotte v. Cook, 348 N.C. 222, 225, 498 S.E.2d 605, 608 (1998).

100. Vance County v. Royster, 271 N.C. 53, 60, 155 S.E.2d 790, 795 (1967) (citations omitted).

101. Transcontinental Gas Pipeline Corp. v. Calco Enterprises, 132 N.C. App. 237, 245, 511 S.E.2d 671, 677 (1999).

102. City of Charlotte v. McNeely, 281 N.C. 684, 690, 190 S.E.2d 179, 184 (1972).

interest to be acquired in the needed property, whether it is ownership in fee or a limited easement right.[103]

North Carolina's courts presume that public officials act in good faith and according to applicable laws and regulations.[104] The court of appeals described the degree of judicial scrutiny over decisions about property to be acquired as follows:

> Although the propriety of a taking is generally not reviewable by the courts once a public purpose is established, our courts have consistently held that "[u]pon specific allegations tending to show bad faith, malice, wantonness, or oppressive and manifest abuse of discretion by the condemnor, [the takings] issue . . . becomes a subject of judicial inquiry as a question of fact to be determined by the judge." Our courts have also held that in raising such allegations, the burden of proof is upon the condemnee to show that an abuse of discretion has indeed occurred as there is a presumption in this State that public officials discharge their duties in good faith and in accordance with the spirit and purpose of the law.[105]

Notwithstanding the broad discretion afforded to local governments to determine the property needed for a public project, Chapter 40A contains certain express constraints regarding local government exercise of eminent domain for acquiring an entire parcel or building when the condemnor's intended use only requires a portion of that parcel or building. G.S. 40-A7 provides that "[w]hen the proposed project requires condemnation of only a portion of a parcel of land leaving a remainder of such shape, size or condition that it is of little value, a condemnor may acquire the entire parcel by purchase or condemnation."[106] The condemnor has the threshold burden of establishing that the remainder is "of little value."[107] In addition to meeting this burden,

---

103. City of Charlotte v. Cook, 348 N.C. 222, 225–27, 498 S.E.2d 605, 607–9 (1998).

104. Bd. of Educ. of Hickory Admin. School Unit v. Seagle, 120 N.C. App. 566, 571, 463 S.E.2d 277, 281 (1995).

105. City of Monroe v. W.F. Harris Dev., LLC, 131 N.C. App. 22, 24–25, 505 S.E.2d 160, 162 (1998) (quoting Greensboro–High Point Airport Auth. v. Irvin, 36 N.C. App. 662, 665, 245 S.E.2d 390, 392, *appeal dismissed*, 295 N.C. 548, 248 S.E.2d 726 (1978), *cert. denied*, 440 U.S. 912 (1979) (citations omitted)).

106. G.S. 40A-7(a).

107. Piedmont Triad Regional Water Auth. v. Sumner Hills Inc., 353 N.C. 343, 346–47, 543 S.E.2d 844, 847 (2001).

the condemnor must allege in the complaint and be prepared to establish that one of the following conditions exists: "[A] partial taking of the land would substantially destroy the economic value or utility of the remainder," "an economy in the expenditure of public funds will be promoted by taking the entire parcel," or "the interest of the public will be best served by acquiring the entire parcel."[108] When the eminent domain acquisition involves a portion of a building, the complaint must recite that the condemnor has determined one of the following conditions exists: "[A]n economy in the expenditure of public funds will be promoted by acquiring the entire building or structure"; "it is not feasible to cut off a portion of the building or structure without destroying the whole"; or "the convenience, safety, or improvement of the project will be promoted by acquiring the entire building or structure."[109] The condemnor is not required to integrate the remainder of the land or building acquired into the project and is free to sell it or exchange it for other property.[110]

1.7 Chapter 40A Eminent Domain Powers of Municipalities and Counties

Most purposes for which local governments may exercise eminent domain are listed in G.S 40A-3. Other statutes confirm municipal and county eminent domain authority to use eminent domain powers entrusted to them for particular purposes.[111]

---

108. G.S. 40A-7(a)(1)–(3); *see Sumner Hills Inc.*, 353 N.C. at 347, 543 S.E.2d at 847–48 (condemnor has burden of affirmatively establishing that the proposed condemnation of remaining property is authorized because it meets one of the conditions in G.S. 40A-7(a)).

109. G.S. 40A-7(c).

110. G.S. 40A-7(b).

111. G.S. 160A-240.1 provides as follows: "A city may acquire, by gift, grant, devise, bequest, exchange, purchase, lease, or any other lawful method, the fee or any lesser interest in real or personal property for use by the city or any department, board, commission or agency of the city. In exercising the power of eminent domain a city shall use the procedures of Chapter 40A." G.S. 153A-158 gives similar authority to counties, by providing as follows: "A county may acquire, by gift, grant, devise, bequest, exchange, purchase, lease, or any other lawful method, the fee or any lesser interest in real or personal property for use by the county or any department, board, commission, or agency of the county. In exercising the power of eminent domain a county shall use the procedures of Chapter 40A."

1.7.1 All Municipalities and Counties

Municipalities and counties have eminent domain power for the following purposes:

- Opening, widening, extending, or improving roads, streets, alleys, and sidewalks[112]
- Establishing, enlarging, or improving parks, playgrounds, and other recreational facilities[113]
- Establishing, extending, enlarging, or improving storm sewer and drainage systems and works or sewer and septic tank lines and systems[114]
- Establishing, enlarging, or improving hospital facilities, cemeteries, or library facilities[115]

G.S. 153A-263 also authorizes both municipalities and counties to use eminent domain to acquire real property for public library systems. G.S. 153A-178 provides that a county may use its eminent domain powers to acquire land for a state psychiatric hospital, and the county may convey it to the state.

Municipalities and counties also have eminent domain powers for the following purposes:

- Constructing, enlarging, or improving city halls, fire stations, office buildings, courthouse jails, and other buildings for use by any department, board, commission, or agency[116]
- Establishing drainage programs and programs to prevent obstructions to the natural flow of streams, creeks, and natural water channels, or improving drainage facilities[117]
- Acquiring historic property designated as such before October 1, 1989, or acquiring a landmark designated as such on or after October 1, 1989, for which an application has been made for a certificate of appropriateness for demolition, in pursuance of the purposes of

---

112. G.S. 40A-3(b)(1).
113. G.S. 40A-3(b)(3).
114. G.S. 40A-3(b)(4).
115. G.S. 40A-3(b)(5).
116. G.S. 40A-3(b)(6).
117. G.S. 40A-3(b)(7).

G.S. 160A-399.3, Chapter 160A, Article 19, Part 3B, effective until October 1, 1989, or G.S. 160A-400.14, whichever is appropriate[118]
- Opening, widening, extending, or improving public wharves[119]
- Establishing, extending, enlarging, or improving any of the public enterprises listed in G.S. 160A-311 for cities or G.S. 153A-274 for counties[120]

The "public enterprises" for which both municipalities and counties are authorized to use eminent domain powers under Chapter 40A are the following:[121]

- Airports[122]
- Off-street parking facilities[123]
- Public transportation systems
- Solid waste collection and disposal systems and facilities
- Stormwater management programs designed to protect water quality by controlling the level of pollutants in, and the quantity and flow

---

118. G.S. 40A-3(b)(8).

119. G.S. 40A-3(b)(9).

120. G.S. 40A-3(b)(2).

121. G.S. 153A-274 (counties); G.S. 160A-311 (municipalities).

122. *See also* G.S. 63-6 (authorizing municipalities and counties to use eminent domain to acquire property needed for an airport or landing field); G.S. 63-49(a) (authorizing municipalities to use eminent domain for airports, and G.S. 63-1(14) defines "municipalities" to include counties as well as cities and towns). Under G.S. 63-49 property previously acquired by an agency or corporation with eminent domain power may be acquired for airport purposes "when such right is exercised on the approach zone or on the airport site," except for property used as railroads or railroad bridges. G.S. 63-49(b). G.S. 63-49 also authorizes municipalities and counties to acquire necessary air space easements, interests in airport hazards, and "other airport protection privileges as are necessary to insure safe approaches to the landing areas of said airports or restricted landing areas and the safe and efficient operation thereof," as well as property needed for placing and maintaining airport-related lights and marks. G.S. 63-49(c).

123. The statute defining municipal enterprises refers to "[o]ff-site parking facilities *and systems*" (G.S. 160A-311(8) (emphasis added)); the statute defining county enterprises refers to "[o]ff-site parking facilities" without mention of "systems" (G.S. 153A-274(5)). There is no reason to believe that a material difference in the scope of authorized purposes is intended.

of, stormwater; and structural and natural stormwater and drainage systems of all types

- Water supply and distribution systems
- Wastewater collection, treatment, and disposal systems of all types, including septic tank systems or other on-site collection or disposal facilities or systems

1.7.2 Municipalities

In addition to the authorized purposes described in section 1.7.1 above, municipalities—not counties—have eminent domain power for the following purposes, which are identified as municipal "public enterprises" for which Chapter 40A authorizes use of eminent domain:[124]

- Cable television systems
- Electric power generation, transmission, and distribution systems
- Gas production, storage, transmission, and distribution systems, where systems also include the purchase or lease of natural gas fields and natural gas reserves; the purchase of natural gas supplies; and the surveying, the drilling, and any other activities related to the exploration for natural gas, whether in or outside the state

Cities may use the same eminent domain powers given by statute to housing authorities for the authorities' authorized purposes, which are described in section 1.8.4 below, either as a city or through a designated housing authority.[125] Cities also are authorized to use the same eminent domain powers given to urban redevelopment commissions for the commissions' authorized purposes, described in section 1.8.9 below, either as a city or through a designated redevelopment commission.[126]

1.7.3 Counties

In addition to the authorized purposes described in section 1.7.1 above, counties are granted eminent domain authority "to acquire property for use by a school administrative unit within the county only upon the request of the board of education of that school administrative unit and after a public

---

124. G.S. 40A-3(b)(2); G.S. 160A-311.
125. G.S. 157-4.1; G.S. 160A-456(b).
126. G.S. 160A-456(b).

hearing."[127] Counties may also use eminent domain to acquire real property for use by a community college "upon request of the board of trustees of the community college for which property is to be made available," in which case the county commissioners must hold a public hearing prior to final action with public notice given of the hearing at least ten days before the hearing is held.[128]

Counties may use the same eminent domain powers given by statute to housing authorities for the authorities' authorized purposes, which are described in section 1.8.4 below, either as a county or through a designated housing authority.[129] Counties also are authorized to use the same eminent domain powers given to urban redevelopment commissions for the commissions' authorized purposes, described in section 1.8.9 below, either as a county or through a designated redevelopment commission.[130]

1.7.4 Coastal Counties and Municipalities

Carteret and Dare counties and a number of coastal communities[131] also have eminent domain power for the following two purposes:

- Engaging in or participating with other governmental entities in acquiring, constructing, reconstructing, extending, or otherwise building or improving beach erosion control or flood and hurricane protection works, including, but not limited to, the acquisition of any property that may be required as a source for beach renourishment[132]
- Establishing access for the public to public trust beaches and appurtenant parking areas[133]

---

127. G.S. 153A-158.1.
128. G.S. 153A-158.2.
129. G.S. 153A-376(b).
130. *Id.*
131. The towns of Atlantic Beach, Carolina Beach, Caswell Beach, Emerald Isle, Holden Beach, Indian Beach, Kill Devil Hills, Kitty Hawk, Kure Beach, Nags Head, North Topsail Beach, Oak Island, Ocean Isle Beach, Pine Knoll Shores, Sunset Beach, Surf City, Topsail Beach, and Wrightsville Beach, and the Village of Bald Head Island. G.S. 40A-3(b1).
132. G.S. 40A-3(b1)(10).
133. G.S. 40A-3(b1)(11).

1.8 Other Local Public Authorities with Eminent Domain Powers under Chapter 40A

The statutes authorize a number of local public agencies and other entities to use eminent domain to acquire property for their authorized purposes. Most of these agencies and entities are listed in Chapter 40A, but some statutes authorizing the creation of certain authorities also provide for eminent domain powers. The following are condemnors authorized in Chapter 40A to use eminent domain.

1.8.1 Community College Trustees

The boards of trustees of North Carolina's community colleges have the power of eminent domain[134] for community college purposes.[135] They may acquire land, easements, and rights-of-way "necessary for proper operation" of community college facilities.[136] As described in section 1.7.3 above, counties may also use eminent domain powers under Chapter 40A to acquire real property for use by a community college "upon request of the board of trustees of the community college for which property is to be made available."[137]

1.8.2 Federal Housing Projects

North Carolina state law authorizes federal housing agencies and federal programs financing housing projects[138] to use eminent domain to acquire real property, fixtures, and improvements for their housing projects.[139] The agency or corporation must first adopt a "resolution declaring that the acquisition of the property described therein is in the public interest and necessary for public use."[140]

1.8.3 Hospital Authorities

Cities and counties may establish hospital authorities to provide hospitals and medical care, and the authorities may use eminent domain[141] to acquire

---

134. G.S. 40A-3(c)(11).

135. G.S. 115-D20(3). State Board of Community Colleges approval may be required. See *id.*

136. *Id.*

137. G.S. 153A-158.2.

138. G.S. 40A-3(c)(6).

139. G.S. 157-50.

140. *Id.*

141. G.S. 40A-3(c)(3).

land, fixtures, and improvements for these facilities.[142] The hospital authority must first obtain a certificate of public convenience and necessity from the North Carolina Utilities Commission for the facility for which the property is to be taken.[143] The authority may not take public, religious, or charitable property without the owner's consent, and no property belonging to a public utility corporation may be acquired without the approval of the authority regulating the utility.[144] The statutes authorize hospital authorities to lease or convey facilities made possible through eminent domain to private individuals or entities.[145]

1.8.4 Housing Authorities

A housing authority organized under Article 1 of Chapter 157 has eminent domain power[146] to acquire real property, fixtures, and improvements for low- and moderate-income housing projects.[147] Before using eminent domain to acquire property, the housing authority must adopt a resolution declaring that the acquisition "is in the public interest and necessary for public use."[148] The statutes also provide that eminent domain may not be used for municipal housing projects unless a certificate of public convenience and necessity is obtained from the North Carolina Utilities Commission.[149] The housing authority may not take public property without the consent of the jurisdiction in which the property is situated, and the authority may not take public utility property without prior approval of the authority regulating the utility.[150]

1.8.5 Mosquito Control Districts

A county, or more than one county or parts of them, may form a mosquito control district, which may use eminent domain[151] to acquire property, easements, and rights-of-way for drainage, filling, diking, or other treatment to control mosquitoes "and other anthropods of public health significance."[152]

---

142. G.S. 131E-15, -17, -24(a).
143. G.S. 131E-24(c).
144. G.S. 131E-24(b).
145. G.S. 131E-23(20), (36).
146. G.S. 40A-3(c)(5).
147. G.S. 157-11.
148. *Id.*
149. G.S. 157-28; G.S. 157-45.
150. G.S. 40A-3(c)(5); G.S. 157-11.
151. G.S. 40A-3(c)(2).
152. G.S. 130A-352, -355(6).

1.8.6 Regional Public Transportation Authorities

Regional public transportation authorities formed under Article 26 of Chapter 160A of the General Statutes have eminent domain power[153] to acquire real and personal property "for use by the Authority."[154] The purpose of regional public transportation authorities is to finance, provide, operate, and maintain terminals, buses, and other transportation facilities, and the statutes authorize the authorities to enter into contracts for operation with, and to lease facilities to, public and private individuals and entities.[155]

1.8.7 Sanitary District Boards

Sanitary districts may be formed across county and municipal boundaries for sewage management, refuge collection, water supply, fire protection, ambulance provision, cemeteries, medical clinics, and other specified public health services.[156] Sanitary district boards have eminent domain power[157] to acquire real estate, easements, and rights-of-way for authorized purposes.[158]

1.8.8 School Boards

Several statutes address the use of eminent domain for educational purposes. G.S. 40A-3(b) provides that "[t]he board of education of any municipality or county or a combined board may exercise the power of eminent domain under [Chapter 40A] for purposes authorized by Chapter 115C of the General Statutes." G.S. 115-C517 authorizes boards of education to acquire sites within or outside their administrative boundaries for school buildings, parking areas, bus access roads, and other school facilities, but the statute provides that the boards may not operate schools outside the unit's administrative boundaries. A board of education must make a determination that it is necessary for the aforementioned purposes to take the land by eminent domain.[159] The statute says that a school board's determination of necessity "shall be conclusive."[160] As described in section 1.6 above, the courts generally defer to the government's determination of necessity unless the owner can demonstrate arbitrariness or

---

153. G.S. 40A-3(c)(13).
154. G.S. 160A-619(a).
155. G.S. 160A-610.
156. G.S. 130A-47, -48, -55.
157. G.S. 40A-3(c)(1).
158. G.S. 130A-57.
159. G.S. 115C-517.
160. *Id.*

bad faith. The North Carolina Court of Appeals interpreted the statutory empowerment of school boards to designate the necessary land as subject to this standard, stating that "the courts are bound by the discretionary decision of a local board of education in selecting and determining the land necessary to construct a school, school building, school bus garage, a parking area, an access road suitable for school buses or 'other school facilities' unless that decision is an 'arbitrary abuse of discretion or disregard of law.'"[161] The court further explained that "[a] discretionary act is an arbitrary abuse of discretion when it is 'not done according to reason or judgment, but depending upon the will alone' and 'done without reason.'"[162]

1.8.9 Urban Redevelopment Commissions

An urban redevelopment commission formed within a municipality according to Article 22 of Chapter 160A has eminent domain power[163] only to acquire property fitting the statutory definition of "blighted parcel."[164] A parcel is "blighted" if a planning commission determines that a residential parcel

> by reason of dilapidation, deterioration, age or obsolescence, inadequate provision for ventilation, light, air, sanitation, or open spaces, high density of population and overcrowding, unsanitary or unsafe conditions, or the existence of conditions which endanger life or property by fire and other causes, or any combination of such factors, substantially impairs the sound growth of the community, is conducive to ill health, transmission of disease, infant mortality, juvenile delinquency and crime, and is detrimental to the public health, safety, morals or welfare.[165]

1.8.10 Water and Sewer Local Government Organizations

As described in section 1.7 above, municipalities and counties have eminent domain power to take property for water and sewer systems, which are basic local

---

161. Dare County Bd. of Educ. v. Sakaria, 118 N.C. App. 609, 615, 456 S.E.2d 842, 846 (1995) (quoting Burlington City Bd. of Educ. v. Allen, 243 N.C. 520, 523, 91 S.E.2d 180, 183 (1956)) (decided based on a prior version of the statute that limited a board's discretion to decisions about sites no larger than fifty acres).

162. *Id.* (quoting *In re* Housing Auth., 235 N.C. 463, 468, 70 S.E.2d 500, 503 (1952)).

163. G.S. 40A-3(c)(7).

164. G.S. 160A-515.

165. G.S. 160A-503(2a).

government enterprises. Chapter 162A gives eminent domain power to other local government organizations formed to provide water or sewer systems;[166] these organizations can consist of a single political subdivision or a consortium of more than one. The organizations granted the power of eminent domain to take land and interests in land for water or sewer systems include water and sewer system authorities organized under Article 1 of Chapter 162A,[167] metropolitan water districts organized under Article 4 of Chapter 162A,[168] metropolitan sewer districts organized under Article 5 of Chapter 162A,[169] and county water and sewer districts organized under Article 6 of Chapter 162A.[170] Sanitary district boards, which may also perform water and sewer functions, have eminent domain powers as described in section 1.8.7 above.

1.8.11 Watershed Improvement Districts

Watershed districts are formed within or across county boundaries based on a determination of need for soil and water conservation by the North Carolina Soil and Water Conservation Commission and a voter referendum.[171] G.S. 40A-3(c)(4) grants eminent domain power to such districts for the purposes stated in the enabling statutes "provided, however, that the provisions of G.S. 139-38 shall continue to apply." The proviso, G.S. 139-38, which was repealed in 1993,[172] had required that watershed improvement districts obtain a finding by the Soil and Water Conservation Commission that a proposed acquisition would be used for a proper district purpose. Current G.S. 139-44 provides that this eminent domain power resides in the counties, subject to the same condition of a Soil and Water Conservation Commission determination of proper purpose. Consequently, the current statutes still list watershed improvement districts as having eminent

---

166. G.S. 40A-3(c)(8), (9), (10), (12).

167. G.S. 40A-3(c)(8); G.S. 162A–6(10). The statute specifying the extent of eminent domain powers for water and sewer authorities mentions "water rights" among the property interests that may be condemned. The other water and sewer statutes do not specifically mention rights in water. This difference is most likely merely stylistic, as private water rights are considered an interest in real property under North Carolina law. Smith v. Town of Morganton, 187 N.C. 801, 803, 123 S.E. 88, 89 (1924).

168. G.S. 40A-3(c)(9); G.S. 162A–36(10).

169. G.S. 40A-3(c)(10); G.S. 162A–69(10).

170. G.S. 40A-3(c)(12); G.S. 162A–89.1.

171. G.S. 139-5.

172. 1993 N.C. Sess. Laws ch. 391, sec. 24.

domain power under Chapter 40A but also indicate that eminent domain proceedings in connection with such programs should be undertaken by counties. This statutory inconsistency likely has no practical effect because the few watershed districts in North Carolina appear to reflect county boundaries.[173]

1.9 Other Local Government Authorities Having Eminent Domain Powers

Other authorities or districts are given eminent domain power in their authorization statutes but are not listed among the public condemnors in Chapter 40A who have eminent domain for purposes stated in that chapter. G.S. 40A-1(a) says that Chapter 40A includes the exclusive list of uses or purposes for which eminent domain may be exercised. It does not say that no other authorities granted power under the statutes may use eminent domain for the same uses or purposes for which counties or municipalities are granted eminent domain power under Chapter 40A. Some statutes expressly state that certain agencies do *not* have the power of eminent domain.[174]

1.9.1 Joint Municipal Electrical Power Projects

Joint agencies formed by municipalities for electric power projects have eminent domain power to be exercised according to the procedures in Chapter 40A, except that the agency may take or cross existing power facilities only after receiving approval in a proceeding before the North Carolina Utilities Commission.[175]

1.9.2 Public Landings

County commissioners may establish "public landings" on navigable streams or watercourses in their counties. The statute requires that the owner of land to be taken for this purpose be given twenty days' prior notice of the

---

173. North Carolina Department of Environment and Natural Resources, Division of Soil and Water Conservation, Map of State Association Areas, www.enr .state.nc.us/DSWC/images/map3.jpg (last visited March 27, 2008).

174. *E.g.*, G.S. 153A-395(9a) (regional planning commissions); G.S. 159C-20 (county industrial facilities and pollution control financing authorities).

175. G.S. 159B-33.

commissioners' intent, and the notice must be posted at the courthouse door. If at the hearing the board determines that there is sufficient reason to establish the landing, it may commence an eminent domain proceeding under Chapter 40A.[176]

1.9.3 Public Transportation Authorities

Public transportation authorities formed under Article 27 of Chapter 160A of the General Statutes, which are similar in function to regional transportation authorities described in section 1.8.6 above but are authorized by separate statutes, have eminent domain power to acquire real and personal property "for use by the Authority."[177] The purpose of public transportation authorities is to finance, provide, operate, and maintain terminals, buses, and other transportation facilities, and the statutes provide that these authorities may enter into contracts for operation with, and to lease the facilities to, public and private individuals and entities.[178]

1.9.4 Regional Natural Gas Districts

One county or municipality or any combination of these may form a regional natural gas district to develop and operate a natural gas system. The statutes provide that the district may employ eminent domain to acquire property interests for district use by following the procedures in Chapter 40A.[179] Before a final judgment can be entered conveying property to a regional natural gas district, the district must obtain the consent of the county board of commissioners of the county in which the land is located.[180]

1.9.5 Regional Solid Waste Management Authorities

Two or more local governmental units may form a regional authority to manage solid waste. The statutes provide that these authorities may employ eminent domain to acquire property within a member's territorial jurisdiction by

---

176. G.S. 77-11. Neither Chapter 40A nor the other statutes listing general county and municipal functions include "public landings" as among the purposes authorized for eminent domain, but G.S. 77-11 was retained when Chapter 40A was enacted in 1981 and its form amended to specify the Chapter 40A procedure. 1981 N.C. Sess. Laws ch. 919, sec. 10.

177. G.S. 160A-649.

178. G.S. 160A-639.

179. G.S. 160A-674.

180. G.S. 160A-674(b).

using the authority granted to counties generally, which would be according to the procedures in Chapter 40A.[181]

1.9.6 Revenue Bond Projects

Municipalities have statutory eminent domain power for revenue bond projects.[182] The authority extends to revenue bond projects involving the kinds of facilities and systems for which eminent domain powers are authorized under other statutes, as well as facilities for use by any federal agency.[183] Eminent domain may be used in connection with revenue bonds for economic development only if the Local Government Commission approved the bonds for the project prior to August 15, 2006.[184]

1.9.7 Special Airport Districts

Local governments may form special airport districts to support and finance airport facilities, and the statutes provide that the districts may acquire rights in land and convey them to government units and airport authorities through the exercise of eminent domain.[185] Special airport districts are not among the public condemnors identified in Chapter 40A as having eminent domain powers, but, as described in section 1.7.1 above, airports are authorized purposes for counties and municipalities.

1.9.8 State Highway System Streets

Municipalities may use the eminent domain authority and procedures authorized for use by the North Carolina Department of Transportation under Chapter 136 to acquire land for a road that will be part of the state highway system pursuant to an agreement between the municipality and the state.[186] As described in section 1.10 below, the method of determining compensation may be different in a Chapter 136 proceeding than what is required under Chapter 40A.

---

181. G.S. 153A-427(23).
182. G.S. 159-83(a)(1).
183. G.S. 159-81(3).
184. G.S. 159-83(a)(1).
185. G.S. 63-83(5).
186. G.S. 136-66.3.

1.10 Eminent Domain Power Conferred by Local Acts

A local act is legislation "operating only in a limited territory or specified locality."[187] For almost a century, the General Assembly commonly used local acts to authorize specific activity by individual local governments. In 1916, amendments to the North Carolina Constitution were ratified to prohibit the General Assembly from enacting any local, private, or special legislation regarding fourteen subjects.[188] This limitation greatly reduced the number of bills the General Assembly enacted to address local issues.[189] However, the General Assembly continued to use local acts extensively for eminent domain until 1981, when the statutes were revised to authorize local governments and authorities to use eminent domain for basic public purposes. Still, the General Assembly continued to enact local legislation to authorize eminent domain for certain public purposes not already approved for the use of eminent domain. A 1985 law, for example, authorized Asheville and Raleigh to use eminent domain to acquire open spaces.[190] In 1985 Wake County was authorized to use eminent domain to acquire property for public safety centers, including jails, offices, and emergency medical facilities.[191] Some cities were given eminent domain power to acquire property meeting certain characteristics of vacancy or code noncompliance to provide low- and moderate-income housing.[192] Some local acts authorized eminent domain for very specific purposes, such as a 1993 act authorizing Wrightsville Beach to use eminent domain to acquire property for beach erosion control and flood and hurricane protection works within a certain territory,[193] a 1991 act giving Duplin County the power to acquire a certain area for an industrial park,[194] and a 1995 act authorizing Stanly County to take certain property for an industrial park to be owned and operated by the airport authority.[195] Local

---

187. McIntyre v. Clarkson, 254 N.C. 510, 517, 119 S.E.2d 888, 893 (1961).

188. N.C. CONST. art. II, sec. 24.

189. *McIntyre*, 254 N.C. at 516, 119 S.E.2d at 892.

190. 1985 N.C. Sess. Laws ch. 556.

191. 1985 N.C. Sess. Laws ch. 640.

192. S.L. 2000-89, sec. 1, subsec 7.81 (Charlotte); 1993 N.C. Sess. Laws ch. 658 (Durham); 1989 N.C. Sess. Laws ch. 466 (Greensboro).

193. 1993 N.C. Sess. Laws ch. 187.

194. 1991 N.C. Sess. Laws ch. 390.

195. 1995 N.C. Sess. Laws ch. 342.

governments have also been authorized to use eminent domain to take property for further conveyance to the state; a 2005 law, for example, authorized a town to acquire property by eminent domain to convey to the state for use as a correctional facility.[196]

When a unit of local government considers taking an eminent domain action based on a local act, it must determine whether the authority to do so remains effective. In 2006 the General Assembly declared ineffective any local acts granting eminent domain authority for purposes other than those enumerated in G.S. 40A-3(a), (b), (b1) or (c), unless the eminent domain action for such other purposes was commenced before August 15, 2006.[197] This would mean, for example, that some economic development local acts conferring authority for eminent domain may have been repealed as inconsistent with the limited powers now extended.[198] The General Assembly expressly did not repeal "any provision of a local act limiting the purposes for which the authority to exercise the power of eminent domain may be used."[199]

The General Assembly also has enacted local acts authorizing use of eminent domain procedures other than those available to local governments under Chapter 40A, and such procedural authorization was not repealed by the 2006 legislation. For example, Charlotte is authorized to use the procedure available to the North Carolina Department of Transportation in Article 9, Chapter 136, for acquiring land for streets and highways, water supply and distribution systems, sewage collection and disposal systems, structural and natural stormwater and drainage systems, public transportation systems, and airports.[200] A condemnor should consult the applicable local acts to determine the purposes for which alternative procedures are authorized and any special limitations on exercise of the power.[201]

---

196. S.L. 2005-258.

197. G.S. 40A-1(a).

198. For example, in 1983 Lumberton was given eminent domain authority for "uptown development projects" in the city's central business district for a project that could include a privately owned hotel or office building. 1983 N.C. Sess. Laws ch. 996. Those powers would no longer exist if the eminent domain action had not commenced by August 15, 2006.

199. G.S. 40A-1(a).

200. S.L 2001-304; S.L. 2000-89, sec. 1, subsec. 7.81(a).

201. *See, e.g.,* S.L. 2005-57 (Holly Springs, for water lines and treatment facilities and sewer lines and treatment facilities and opening, widening, extending, or improving public streets and roads); S.L. 2003-327, sec. 1, subsec. 360 (Rocky

Before employing a procedure alternative to those authorized by Chapter 40A, a local government should consider the possible differences in the procedure and in the compensation it would require. For example, the procedure available to the North Carolina Department of Transportation under Chapter 136, which is sometimes available to local governments, does not require that thirty days' advance notice be given to each owner before a complaint is filed, although case law indicates that the complaint must allege that the condemnor attempted in good faith to acquire the property by agreement.[202] Chapter 136 also has a different rule for determining compensation in a partial taking. Under Chapter 136 the owner is entitled to the diminished fair market value of the property remaining after the taking, offset by general and special benefits.[203] The owner does not have the alternative authorized under Chapter 40A of receiving compensation based on the value of the property taken.[204]

Mount, for streets and highways; water supply and distribution systems; sewage collection and disposal systems; electric power generation, transmission and distribution systems; and gas storage, transmission, and distribution systems); S.L. 2003-88 (Apex, for opening, widening, extending, or improving public streets and roads; expires December 31, 2008); 1989 N.C. Sess. Laws ch. 348 (Wilson, for streets and highways; water supply and distribution systems; sewage collection and disposal systems; electric power generation, transmission and distribution systems; and gas storage, transmission and distribution systems); 1987 N.C. Sess. Laws ch. 70 (Apex, for water lines and treatment facilities and sewer lines and treatment facilities); 1985 N.C. Sess. Laws ch. 422 (Conover, Hickory, and Maiden, for streets and highways, water supply and distribution systems, sewage collection and disposal systems, and airports); 1985 N.C. Sess. Laws ch. 47 (Winston-Salem, for streets and highways, water supply and distribution systems, sewage collection and disposal systems, and airports).

202. *See* City of Charlotte v. Robinson, 2 N.C. App. 429, 163 S.E.2d 289 (1968) (holding that allegation of good faith attempt to acquire the property by negotiation is required despite absence of such requirement in the statute). The notice requirement for local government condemnations under Chapter 40A is in G.S. 40A-40(a). As examples of some other significant differences, *see also, e.g.,* G.S. 136-107 (owner has twelve months to answer rather than ninety days as allowed by G.S. 40A-45); G.S. 136-112(1) (the measure of damages for a partial taking is the difference in value for the remainder, without the alternative under G.S. 40A-64 of the fair market value of the property taken).

203. G.S. 136-112(1).

204. G.S. 40A-64.

1.11 Cross-Jurisdictional Eminent Domain

All eminent domain power delegated to counties, municipalities, and local government organizations derives from the authority of the state legislature, and the General Assembly's acts define the limits of permissible exercise of eminent domain. The statutes require most, but not all, local governments and authorities seeking to use eminent domain to acquire land in another county to obtain the consent of the other county's board of commissioners.[205] This requirement varies locally, and government entities should consult current laws to determine whether it applies in any particular contemplated circumstance.[206] The statutes do not require a municipality to obtain county commissioners' consent to acquire land within the municipality's county.

Cross-jurisdictional eminent domain actions may raise other issues as well. For example, a local government acquiring property for wetlands mitigation may be required to compensate another county for loss of future tax revenue for property removed from the tax rolls.[207] Any proposed exercise of eminent domain to acquire property either outside a local government's jurisdiction or held by a utility or other condemnor should proceed only after thorough research of the authority for the acquisition and any specifically applicable restrictions or requirements.

---

205. G.S. 153A-15(a), (b).

206. *See id.* Note, Local Modification (identifying local modifications).

207. G.S. 153A-15.1(a); *see also, e.g.,* G.S. 160A-674(b) (regional gas district cannot acquire land without approval of the board of commissioners of county in which land is located).

2 Local Government Eminent Domain Procedure

2.1   **Overview and Practice Considerations**   **45**

2.2   **Offer to Purchase or Request for Gift**   **47**

2.3   **Dispute Resolution Forum**   **47**

     2.3.1   Alternative Dispute Resolution   48

     2.3.2   Litigation   48

         2.3.2.1   Commissioners   49

         2.3.2.2   Court and Jury   49

2.4   **Rules of Litigation Procedure**   **50**

2.5   **Vesting of Title; Injunctive Relief**   **51**

     2.5.1   Immediate Vesting, or "Quick Take"   51

     2.5.2   Vesting Other than "Quick Take"   53

     2.5.3   Injunctions   53

2.6   **Parties to Eminent Domain Action**   **54**

     2.6.1   Necessary and Proper Parties   55

     2.6.2   Guardians Ad Litem   58

2.7   **Discovery and Proof of Value**   **59**

     2.7.1   Information Discovery and Experts   59

     2.7.2   Witnesses and Other Proof   61

2.8   **Pleadings, Notices, and Other Litigation Requirements**   **64**

     2.8.1   Notice of Intent to Enter Property   65

     2.8.2   Notice of Action   66

     2.8.3   Complaint, Declaration of Taking, and Notice of Deposit   69

2.8.4   Summons and Service   72

2.8.4.1   Summons   72

2.8.4.2   Service   72

2.8.5   Memorandum of Action   73

2.8.6   Condemnor's Plat   75

2.8.7   Answer   76

2.8.8   Reply   77

2.8.9   Deposit and Its Disbursement   77

2.8.10   Appointment of Commissioners   78

2.8.11   Commissioners' Report   81

2.8.12   Notice of Appeal from Commissioners' Report   82

2.9   Abandonment of Project during Proceeding   83

2.10   Judgment and Payment of Compensation   84

2.11   Costs and Attorneys' Fees   92

2.12   Return of Condemned Property   92

2.13   Inverse Condemnation Procedure   93

Forms

Notice of Intent to Enter Property   66

Notice of Action   68

Complaint, Declaration of Taking, and Notice of Deposit   70

Memorandum of Action   74

Motion for Appointment of Commissioners   79

Order Appointing Commissioners   80

Commissioners' Report   81

Exception to Commissioners' Award and Demand for Jury Trial   83

Consent Judgment   85

Motion for Judgment on Commissioners' Award   87

Final Judgment on Commissioners' Award   90

2.1 Overview and Practice Considerations

An eminent domain proceeding is in many ways the same as any other civil case—complying with procedure is essential. Failing to follow the rules can result in delay, lost opportunity, and even dismissal of an action and an obligation to reimburse another party's costs and attorneys' fees. An attorney contemplating an eminent domain action must be familiar with the North Carolina Rules of Civil Procedure as well as the rules and practices of the particular court in which the action is to be filed. In addition, there are required procedures peculiar to eminent domain actions, including the procedures found in Chapter 40A, which apply to most local government condemnations.

Successful navigation of the eminent domain process requires establishing the just compensation to be paid to the owner. The compensation to which the owner is entitled usually is the only seriously contested issue in an eminent domain case. The parties involved in eminent domain actions must collect and coherently present evidence about compensation to support their positions. This requires both familiarity with appraisal methods and an understanding of the nature of real estate ownership interests and property development. An understanding of land use regulations and real estate law also is important to determine an affected parcel's development potential and therefore for preparing and presenting a case about the amount of just compensation. Proper acquisition of property through eminent domain also requires attending to the record of real estate title transfer, which in turn involves making proper recordings at the office of the register of deeds. Attorneys who do not have recent significant experience with eminent domain actions and real estate transactions should consider consulting someone who does.

Persons who understand the eminent domain process and who take positions solidly based on supportive valuations are most likely to achieve their objectives in an eminent domain case. The following is an overview of the major actions in a typical local government condemnation proceeding, which are more fully described below in this chapter. These descriptions are necessarily generalizations; neither this overview nor this book is intended to identify every possible or permissible filing or action.

At least thirty days before filing an eminent domain case, the condemnor must mail the owner a *notice of action*. The notice informs the owner about the condemnor's intent to file a condemnation action and includes the amount the condemnor believes is just compensation the owner will receive for the property. To begin the proceeding, the condemnor files a *complaint, declaration of taking, and notice of deposit*. This document describes the purpose for the acquisition and the property to be acquired and otherwise affected for purposes of compensation. It also describes the legal authority for use of eminent domain and provides the condemnor's assessment of estimated compensation, giving notice that this compensation has been deposited with the court. An owner who will only be contesting the amount of compensation may withdraw from the deposit without losing the right to contest the amount's sufficiency. When the complaint is filed, the condemnor also files a *memorandum of action*, describing the property and the pending action, with the register of deeds. For most purposes the condemnor acquires title and a right to possession at the time the complaint is filed.

The owner responds to the complaint with an *answer*, which must be filed within 120 days after the complaint is served. With this pleading the owner responds to the condemnor's allegations, makes any affirmative claims, and may demand that a jury decide the amount of just compensation. The condemnor then has 90 days to file a *reply*, an optional response to the owner's answer. Within 90 days after receiving the answer, the condemnor must file a *plat* with the court to show the property being acquired and any other property that should be considered in determining just compensation.

During the proceeding the parties will exchange information about their claims and positions, including details about how they value the property being acquired, and may make formal discovery requests that such information be disclosed. The court will decide legal issues, including disputes about what property is being taken, the proper parties, or competing claims to the deposit. The issue of just compensation will be submitted to a jury if a jury was demanded by either party, or the parties can elect to have the issue decided by three appointed commissioners or by the judge. Those who choose to submit the issue to commissioners have a right to challenge the decision and have just compensation newly decided by a jury or the judge. After all the issues have been decided, final judgment will be entered and filed with the register of deeds to reflect the transfer of ownership. The condemnor will pay to the owner any amounts still owed for just compensation to the extent not already paid by withdrawal from the deposit.

2.2 Offer to Purchase or Request for Gift

A local public condemnor filing an eminent domain action under Chapter 40A is not required to make an offer of compensation to the owner of the affected property, though offers and negotiation do not prejudice the condemnor's ability to proceed with eminent domain.[1] A condemnor's offer to acquire property in anticipation of litigation would not be admissible evidence of the property's value in the condemnation proceeding, nor would amounts paid for similar tracts acquired in anticipation of condemnation.[2] G.S. 40A-4 requires a "potential condemnor who seeks to acquire property by gift or purchase" to give the owner written notice of the owner's right to reimbursement of the pro rata portion of paid real estate taxes attributable to the period after title vests in the condemnor.[3] Natural persons owning land taken by eminent domain who also own adjacent agricultural land, horticultural land, or forestland may also be entitled to notice of a right to reimbursement of deferred taxes.[4]

2.3 Dispute Resolution Forum

As explained in section 2.3.2.2 below, the court decides legal questions in an eminent domain proceeding, including questions about a local government's eminent domain power, the necessary parties, the area taken, and other matters except just compensation. If the parties to an eminent domain matter disagree only about the proper amount of compensation to be paid, the dispute can be decided in four different ways: by referral to a third party such as a mediator or in a court proceeding by submission to a panel of three commissioners, a judge, or a jury.

---

1. N.C. Gen. Stat. Ann. § 40A-4 (2007) (hereinafter G.S.).

2. Barnes v. North Carolina State Highway Comm'n, 250 N.C. 378, 396, 109 S.E.2d 219, 233 (1959). Amounts paid for similar tracts acquired in anticipation of condemnation are not considered to reflect what someone would pay as fair market value, absent the threat of condemnation. *Id.*

3. G.S. 40A-4; G.S. 40A-6.

4. G.S. 40A-6(b).

2.3.1   Alternative Dispute Resolution

Before and during litigation, parties to a dispute should consider engaging a mediator to facilitate a discussion and encourage an agreement that avoids the delay, expense, and uncertainty of contested dispute resolution. Mediators do not issue decisions. They invite the parties to exchange information, discuss their interests, and mutually work toward an agreement acceptable to all concerned. Mediation can save everyone considerable expense and enable the parties to devote their time and energy to things more productive than litigation. Because a mediator is a facilitator and not a decision maker, the mediator of an eminent domain matter need not be an expert in real estate valuation, and parties should be able to agree on an attorney, retired judge, or other appropriately trained or experienced individual to conduct the mediation. Courts sometimes require or encourage mediation, but in any event it is usually worthwhile. The following are among the possible advantages of mediation:

- The parties retain control over the outcome because they must agree to the resolution; they do not relinquish that control to commissioners, a judge, or a jury.
- The outcome can be tailored to the parties' needs and interests.
- The parties are free to address all issues of concern to them, not just legal causes of action.
- There is greater likelihood that all of the parties will accept the resolution rather than continue to feel adversely toward each other.
- The process may save significant expense and time.

The parties also could refer the matter to an arbitrator for a binding resolution. Those who choose arbitration usually prefer the process to litigation because of the parties' ability to choose a decision maker who has experience with the kinds of issues involved in the dispute, which in an eminent domain context would include at least basic knowledge about real estate valuation. Use of the statutorily defined procedure for having commissioners determine just compensation can serve this purpose, and arbitration therefore is not common in eminent domain cases.

2.3.2   Litigation

The procedure for eminent domain actions in county superior court can involve three different decision makers: commissioners, judge, and jury.

2.3.2.1 Commissioners

The statutes governing eminent domain procedure provide either party the option of referring the compensation determination to commissioners if requested within sixty days after the answer is filed.[5] An advantage of having commissioners determine valuation is that the parties can choose commissioners who have real estate valuation experience. Such experts may involve significant cost. G.S. 1-408 provides that "the clerk may fix a reasonable fee for the services of the commissioner or commissioners performed under the order or judgment. The fee shall be taxed as part of the costs in the action or proceeding." Usually the condemnor pays the commissioners' fees as part of the costs. The clerk's determination of costs is an appealable issue.[6] Section 2.8.10 below further describes the procedure for use of commissioners.

2.3.2.2 Court and Jury

If the parties do not request appointment of commissioners within sixty days after the answer is filed, the issue of just compensation is transferred to the civil issue docket for trial.[7] The North Carolina Supreme Court has held that owners do not have a constitutional right to have a jury decide the issue of just compensation; such a right exists only when the governing statutory procedure provides for it.[8] Rule of Civil Procedure 38(e) provides that "[t]he right of trial by jury as to the issue of just compensation shall be granted to the parties involved in any condemnation proceeding brought by bodies public, corporations or persons which possess the power of eminent domain."[9] The right to a jury trial is deemed waived if not made in writing and served on the other parties "not later than 10 days after the service of the last pleading directed" to the issue as to which a right to a jury trial exists.[10] Owners commonly make a demand for a jury trial in the answer.

The judge will determine all questions of law. G.S. 40A-47 specifies that the judge may hear and determine "questions of necessary and proper parties, title to the land, interest taken, and area taken" upon motion and with ten

---

5. G.S. 40A-48.

6. G.S. 1-408.

7. G.S. 40A-49.

8. Kaperonis v. North Carolina State Highway Comm'n, 260 N.C. 587, 593–96, 133 S.E.2d 464, 469–71 (1963).

9. G.S. 1A-1, Rule 38(e).

10. G.S. 1A-1, Rule 38(b), (d).

days' notice.[11] Conflicting claims of entitlement to the compensation award are resolved by the judge, including allocation of the amount the condemnor deposited with the court and any additional amount required to equal the amount determined to be just compensation.[12] Chapter 40A provides that "[t]he judge may by further order in the cause direct to whom the same shall be paid and may in its discretion order a reference to ascertain the facts on which such determination and order are to be made."[13]

2.4 Rules of Litigation Procedure

Chapter 40A, which governs most local government eminent domain actions, states that the procedures contained therein "shall be the exclusive condemnation procedures" for local public condemnors.[14] The North Carolina Supreme Court has instructed that G.S. 40A-12 and G.S. 1-393 authorize trial courts to apply the Rules of Civil Procedure "at least to the extent that those rules do not directly conflict with procedures specifically mandated by Chapter 40A."[15] Chapter 40A directs that when neither Chapter 40A nor the Rules of Civil Procedure addresses the proper procedure, "the judge before whom such proceeding may be pending shall have the power to make all the necessary orders and rules of procedure necessary to carry into effect the object and intent of this Chapter. The practice in each such case shall conform as near as may be to the practice in other civil actions."[16]

---

11. A party might have a right to have a jury decide ownership as between competing claimants to title. The North Carolina Supreme Court has said that owners have a constitutional right to a jury trial on questions involving title. Wescott v. State Highway Comm'n, 262 N.C. 522, 526, 138 S.E.2d 133, 136 (1964) (There is a "constitutional guaranty of jury trial when the issue determinative of the rights of the litigants is: 'Who owns the land, plaintiff or defendant?'").

12. G.S. 40A-55.

13. *Id.*

14. G.S. 40A-1.

15. Virginia Elec. and Power Co. v. Tillett, 316 N.C. 73, 77–78, 340 S.E.2d 62, 65 (1986). *Tillett* involved a private condemnation proceeding, but G.S. 40A-12 applies to all actions under Chapter 40A, including those brought by local public condemnors. In *Tillett* the North Carolina Supreme Court held that the trial court properly allowed an amendment of the pleadings to convert a condemnation proceeding into a quiet title action under Rule 15, because there was no conflict between the civil procedure rules on amendments to pleadings and any eminent domain rules of procedure. *Id.* at 77–78, 340 S.E.2d at 64–65.

16. G.S. 40A-12.

2.5 Vesting of Title; Injunctive Relief

A condemnor employing eminent domain seeks to acquire uncontestable title to property. The point at which title vests in the condemnor in a Chapter 40A proceeding depends on the purpose for which the power is being exercised. In most circumstances title vests immediately in the condemnor when the eminent domain complaint is filed, and the litigation is over the amount of compensation that must be paid. In some cases title does not vest until later in the proceeding or, in rare cases, upon a final judgment. To attempt to prevent title from passing automatically upon an event in the proceeding, an owner could file a motion for injunctive relief before the event.

2.5.1 Immediate Vesting, or "Quick Take"

When property is taken for the purposes designated for what is commonly known as the "quick take" procedure, title and the right to immediate possession vests in the condemnor when the complaint is filed. If no injunctive relief has been issued, title vests upon the filing of the complaint when any local public condemnor is acquiring property by condemnation for the following traditional local government services:

- Opening, widening, extending, or improving roads, streets, alleys, and sidewalks[17]
- Establishing, extending, enlarging, or improving storm sewer and drainage systems and works or sewer and septic tank lines and systems[18]
- Establishing drainage programs and programs to prevent obstructions to the natural flow of streams, creeks, and natural water channels or improving drainage facilities[19]
- Solid waste collection and disposal systems and facilities[20]
- Water supply and distribution systems[21]
- Wastewater collection, treatment, and disposal systems of all types, including septic tank systems or other on-site collection or disposal facilities or systems[22]

---

17. G.S. 40A-42(a)(1); G.S. 40A-3(b)(1).
18. G.S. 40A-42(a)(1); G.S. 40A-3(4).
19. G.S. 40A-42(a)(1); G.S. 40A-3(7).
20. G.S. 40A-42(a)(1); G.S. 153A-274(3); G.S. 160A-311(6).
21. G.S. 40A-42(a)(1); G.S. 153A-274(1); G.S. 160A-311(2).
22. G.S. 40A-42(a)(1); G.S. 153A-274(2); G.S. 160A-311(3).

Title vests immediately upon the filing of a complaint if Carteret or Dare County or specified coastal communities[23] use eminent domain for the following additional two purposes:

- Engaging or participating with other governmental entities in acquiring, constructing, reconstructing, extending, or otherwise building or improving beach erosion control or flood and hurricane protection works, including, but not limited to, the acquisition of any property that may be required as a source for beach renourishment[24]
- Establishing access for the public to public trust beaches and appurtenant parking areas[25]

The same immediate vesting upon filing of the complaint applies when a municipality is acquiring property for the following purposes:

- Cable television systems[26]
- Electric power generation, transmission, and distribution systems[27]
- Gas production, storage, transmission, and distribution systems, where systems also include the purchase or lease of natural gas fields and natural gas reserves; the purchase of natural gas supplies; and the surveying, drilling and any other activities related to the exploration for natural gas, whether inside or outside the state[28]

---

23. The towns of Atlantic Beach, Carolina Beach, Caswell Beach, Emerald Isle, Holden Beach, Indian Beach, Kill Devil Hills, Kitty Hawk, Kure Beach, Nags Head, North Topsail Beach, Oak Island, Ocean Isle Beach, Pine Knoll Shores, Sunset Beach, Surf City, Topsail Beach, and Wrightsville Beach; and the Village of Bald Head Island. G.S. 40A-3(b1).
24. G.S. 40A-42(a)(2); G.S. 40A-3(b1)(10).
25. G.S. 40A-42(a)(2); G.S. 40A-3(b1)(11).
26. G.S. 40A-42(a)(1); G.S. 160A-311(7).
27. G.S. 40A-42(a)(1); G.S. 160A-311(1).
28. G.S. 40A-42(a)(1); G.S. 160A-311(4).

Title vests immediately upon the filing of a complaint by the following entities for their authorized purposes:

- Boards of education, to acquire sites for school buildings, parking areas, bus access roads, and other school facilities[29]
- Water and sewer authorities organized under Article 1 of Chapter 162A[30]
- Metropolitan water districts[31]
- Metropolitan sewer districts[32]
- County water and sewer districts[33]
- Regional public transportation authorities formed by counties[34]

2.5.2 Vesting Other than "Quick Take"

If property is being taken for purposes other than those specified for immediate vesting as described in the preceding section, unless injunctive relief has been granted, title vests upon occurrence of any of the following three events: when the answer is filed, if only compensation is contested; upon the failure to file an answer within the required time limit; or upon disbursement of the deposit.[35] However, if property is taken from a private condemnor, title does not vest until a final judgment determines that the property is not in "actual public use" or necessary for the business of the private condemnor having title to the property.[36] In cases not involving immediate vesting or vesting upon one of the three events listed above in this paragraph, title would vest upon a final judgment or as of an earlier date specified by the court (as might occur, for example, if a court determines that injunctive relief should not have been granted).

2.5.3 Injunctions

The statute describing immediate vesting states that its provisions "shall not preclude or otherwise affect any remedy of injunction available to the owner or the condemnor."[37] The statute further provides that title vests upon any of

---

29. G.S. 40A-42(a)(2); G.S. 115C-517.
30. G.S. 40A-42(a)(1); G.S. 40A-3(c)(8).
31. G.S. 40A-42(a)(1); G.S. 40A-3(c)(9).
32. G.S. 40A-42(a)(1); G.S. 40A-3(c)(10).
33. G.S. 40A-42(a)(1); G.S. 40A-3(c)(12).
34. G.S. 40A-42(a)(1); G.S. 40A-3(c)(13).
35. G.S. 40A-42(b).
36. G.S. 40A-42(c).
37. G.S. 40A-42(f).

the events described in the preceding section "[u]nless an action for injunctive relief has been initiated."[38] In *Nelson v. Town of Highlands*,[39] the North Carolina Supreme Court confirmed that Chapter 40A preserved the availability of injunctive relief to owners and condemnors.

A condemnor may be required to give an owner notice of the availability of injunctive relief before filing an eminent domain action. As described in section 2.8.2 below, G.S. 40A-40 requires that a public condemnor proceeding under Chapter 40A must give each owner of the subject property, whose name and address can be ascertained by reasonable diligence, written notice of the action at least thirty days before the complaint is filed. If the condemnation is a "quick take" under G.S. 40A-42, the notice must also advise the owner of "[t]he right to commence an action for injunctive relief," among other things.[40] The notice's required contents are described in section 2.8.2 below.

If an owner appeals a judgment directing that real property be delivered to the condemnor, to obtain an injunction against delivery pending appeal the owner must post a bond in an amount fixed by the trial court.[41]

2.6   Parties to Eminent Domain Action

Successful consummation of an acquisition of property through eminent domain requires that all necessary parties be given any required notice of the proceeding. Any issues about who has a right to claim compensation may have to be decided before the question of just compensation can be addressed. As the North Carolina Supreme Court explained, "Whenever . . . a fatal defect of parties is disclosed, the Court should refuse to deal with the merits of the case until the absent parties are brought into the action, and in the absence of a proper motion by a competent person, the defect should be corrected by *ex mero motu* ruling of the Court."[42] Local governments therefore should

---

38. G.S. 40A-42(a), (b).

39. 358 N.C. 210, 594 S.E.2d 21 (2004) (adopting Nelson v. Town of Highlands, 159 N.C. App. 393, 399–400, 583 S.E.2d 313, 317 (2004) (Hudson, J., dissenting)).

40. G.S. 40A-40(b).

41. G.S. 1-292.

42. Town of Morganton v. Hutton & Bourbonnais Co., 247 N.C. 666, 668, 101 S.E.2d 679, 682 (1969); *see also* North Carolina State Highway Comm'n v. Gamble, 6 N.C. App. 568, 571, 170 S.E.2d 359, 361 (1969) ("When it appears, as here, in a

carefully examine the real estate records and other available information, as well as the law governing rights to compensation, to identify the appropriate named defendants.

2.6.1 Necessary and Proper Parties

Condemnation actions sometimes involve disputes about who holds property interests for which compensation must be paid as well as to whom notice of the action must be given. North Carolina statutes governing eminent domain actions by local governments, General Statutes Chapter 40A, take a broad approach with respect to those entitled to be included in the proceeding. The chapter defines an *owner* as "any person having an interest or estate in the property."[43] It also broadly defines *property* as "any right, title, or interest in land, including leases and options to buy or sell. 'Property' also includes rights of access, rights-of-way, easements, water rights, air rights, and any other privilege or appurtenance in or to the possession, use, and enjoyment of land."[44] Accordingly, in addition to those who hold title as owners of the property as that term is commonly understood, an "owner" for purposes of eminent domain would also include the holders of a wide variety of real estate interests, including those with options to purchase, easement holders, lessees, and deed of trust beneficiaries. To ensure that all appropriate parties are included, a condemnor must consider the law governing real estate ownership interests.

Real estate ownership rights largely depend on public records of conveyances. The register of deeds maintains the official record of real estate ownership interests. North Carolina has a "pure" race recording statute, which provides that no deed or other instrument of conveyance "shall be valid to pass any property interest as against lien creditors or purchasers for a valuable consideration from the donor, bargainor or lessor but from the time of registration thereof in the county where the land lies."[45] The real estate records are therefore the primary source of determining ownership interests.

---

case involving the construction of a deed that the absence of a party prevents the entry of a judgment fully settling and determining the question of interpretation, we think the court should refuse to deal with the merits of the case until the absent party is brought in").

43. G.S. 40A-2(5).

44. G.S. 40A-2(7).

45. G.S. 47-18(a) (deeds); G.S. 47-20 (security instruments); G.S. 47-27 (easements).

The question of proper parties in an eminent domain case, however, is not necessarily confined to identification of those who have a recorded ownership interest. In *Transcontinental Gas Pipe Line Co. v. Calco Enterprises*,[46] the North Carolina Court of Appeals held that a month-to-month tenant, who had no recorded lease, had standing in an eminent domain action because the condemnor had *actual* knowledge of the tenant's interest. Actual knowledge is not a consideration in determining ownership rights according to North Carolina's recording statute. The court noted that a month-to-month tenant may not be entitled to compensation based on the value of the lease interest, but also said that the tenant had standing to challenge the proceeding as arbitrary, capricious, or an abuse of discretion.[47] This observation illustrates that someone may be deemed to have the right to participate in an eminent domain proceeding without having a compensable interest in the property being acquired.

The issue of party status is further complicated by the nature of some real estate interests. For example, the eminent domain statutes do not expressly address who has a "right, title or interest in land" in a deed of trust so as to be deemed the land's owner. A deed of trust conveys the property to a trustee to hold for a lender's benefit, and as holder of legal title the trustee would be a necessary party. In *Long v. City of Charlotte*,[48] the North Carolina Supreme Court held that both the trustee and note holder were necessary parties at least when their interests in the property could be impaired as a result of the taking. The court said that in such a case "the trustee and the holder of the note secured by the deed of trust on that property would be vitally interested in having the debt satisfied from the proceeds of the jury verdict."[49] The rights to compensation as between the deed of trust beneficiary and the landowner will depend on various factors, including the terms of the deed of trust and the amount of outstanding indebtedness in relation to the value of the property remaining after the taking. In a Chapter 40A proceeding to acquire part of a tract, a lienholder shares in the awarded compensation "only to the extent determined by the commissioners or by the jury or by the judge to be necessary to prevent an impairment of his security, and the lien shall

---

46. 132 N.C. App. 237, 511 S.E.2d 671 (1999).
47. *Id.* at 241–43, 511 S.E.2d at 675–76.
48. 306 N.C. 187, 293 S.E.2d 101 (1982).
49. *Id.* at 211, 293 S.E.2d at 116.

continue upon the part of the property not taken as security for the unpaid portion of the indebtedness until it is paid."[50] These issues do not affect the total amount of compensation that the condemnor must pay, but they do affect the identification of parties to be included in the proceeding who have the right to claim a share of the compensation.

If a party with an interest in the property to be acquired is the subject of a pending bankruptcy proceeding, federal law may require that the condemnor first obtain bankruptcy court approval before proceeding with the state eminent domain action. The federal Bankruptcy Code prohibits "any act to obtain possession of property of the estate or of property from the estate or to exercise control over property of the estate" without first obtaining bankruptcy court relief from the stay.[51] The bankruptcy court also would be the forum for resolution of disputes about the debtor's interest and distribution of the owner's compensation. Some courts have held that an exception in the Bankruptcy Code from the automatic stay for "the commencement or continuation of an action or proceeding by a government unit . . . to enforce such governmental unit's or organization's police and regulatory power"[52] applies to eminent domain actions. These decisions seem based on the courts' conclusion that the eminent domain power was being used to address an ongoing safety issue, which in the courts' view made the eminent domain action a kind of regulatory enforcement.[53] The Fourth Circuit Court of Appeals recently held, however, that the police and regulatory power exception to the automatic stay does not apply to an eminent domain action, at least when the taking is not aimed at correcting an ongoing public health or safety regulation violation.[54] A condemnor would avoid potential complications in an eminent domain action by asking the bankruptcy court to lift the stay to enable the condemnation proceeding to proceed in state court, with the debtor's condemnation award to be paid to the bankruptcy trustee or otherwise as directed by the bankruptcy court.

---

50. G.S. 40A-68(1).

51. 11 U.S.C. § 362(a)(3) (2000); *id.* § 362(d).

52. *Id.* § 362(b)(4).

53. *See* Bevelle v. Johnson County, 348 B.R. 812, 817–20 (Bankr. N.D. Ala. 2006) (discussing cases and holding that an eminent domain action to take property for a courthouse complying with safety guidelines is a police or regulatory action exempt from the automatic stay).

54. *In re* Royal, 137 Fed. App'x. 537, 539–42 (4th Cir. 2005).

2.6.2 Guardians Ad Litem

Sometimes a party with an ownership interest in property that is the subject of an eminent domain acquisition cannot be identified or located through title research and other reasonable investigation. The statutes provide for use of a guardian ad litem to represent such interests. Chapter 40A provides as follows:

> The judge shall appoint an attorney to appear for and protect the rights of any party or parties in interest who are unknown, or whose residence is unknown and who has not appeared in the proceeding by an attorney or agent. The State Treasurer as custodian of the Escheat Fund shall be notified of the appointment of such an attorney. The judge shall appoint guardians ad litem for such parties as are infants, incompetents, or other parties who may be under a disability, and without general guardian, and the judge shall have the authority to make such additional parties as are necessary to the complete determination of the proceeding.[55]

North Carolina Rule of Civil Procedure 17(d) provides for appointment of a guardian for someone who cannot be ascertained upon the motion of a party "or of other person interested." As quoted above, Chapter 40A requires that service be made on the state treasurer when such an appointment is made. North Carolina Rule of Civil Procedure 17(c) provides for appointment of a guardian for an infant or an insane or incompetent person upon the motion of a party or by the court on its own motion. The North Carolina Supreme Court has held that due process requires that the person for whom a guardian is to be appointed, who has a property right or right to damages, must be given the opportunity to be heard on the question of capacity.[56] Accordingly, a known person for whom a guardian is proposed must be given notice of the proposal, and notice should also be given to any known legal representative of such person.

---

55. G.S. 40A-50.
56. Hagins v. Redevelopment Comm'n of Greensboro, 275 N.C. 90, 165 S.E.2d 490 (1969).

2.7 Discovery and Proof of Value

Unlike some types of litigation, an eminent domain case is unlikely to require resolution of fundamentally contradictory versions of events. Resolution of eminent domain litigation tends to be about reconciling plausible but differing valuations. Most eminent domain disputes involve a contest between appraisers and other experts in real estate valuation and development. The decision maker may accept either party's reasonable valuation or arrive at a compromise or entirely different conclusion based on the facts and testimony. The fact finder is not required to accept any party's valuation as correct or as a limit on the proper amount of just compensation.

2.7.1 Information Discovery and Experts

In some cases, by the time a complaint is filed the condemnor will already know information necessary for pursuing the eminent domain proceeding to its completion. As described in section 2.8.1 below, the statutes authorize a prospective condemnor to enter the land and conduct examinations on it, and the condemnor most likely will have obtained an appraisal or other valuation information or opinions to determine a reasonable amount of just compensation. The condemnor will have shared this information with the owner to enable the owner to assess the fairness of the condemnor's proposal. If the owner disagrees with the valuation, the owner should share the appraisals and other information on which the owner is relying, with the aim of reaching an agreement that avoids the delay, expense, uncertainty, and other costs and risks of litigation. If the matter proceeds to litigation, the parties should consider employing informal requests, or routine interrogatories and production requests if necessary, to obtain the information being used by the other party.

Rule of Civil Procedure 26(b)(4)(a)(1) permits a party to obtain by interrogatories the identity of expert witnesses expected to testify at trial, as well as the subject of that testimony, the facts and opinions about which the witnesses will testify, and a summary of the grounds for their opinions. Occasionally a party believes the other party has information that contradicts a position taken, such as appraisals or reports acquired in connection with the eminent domain proceeding but not intended to be used as evidence at the trial. This may occur, for example, if a party obtains an appraisal but it is unhelpful to the party's case. A party is not clearly entitled to disclosure of information about expert witnesses not intended to be called at trial.

An owner may be entitled to disclosure of information collected by or in behalf of a condemnor based on the public records law, G.S. 132-1. With few exceptions, the public records law allows anyone to obtain copies of documents "made or received pursuant to law or ordinance in connection with the transaction of public business" from governmental units.[57] One exception from the access requirement is for written communications "made within the scope of the attorney–client relationship by any attorney-at-law" representing a governmental unit.[58] An owner's counsel would therefore not be entitled to receive copies of attorney–client privileged communications. The statutory privilege has been construed narrowly to apply only to attorneys' statements to their clients.[59] By statute, confidential attorney–client communications are not public records unless so designated by the governmental body or unless three years have passed since the communication.[60]

Materials collected by an attorney in anticipation of trial are also not discoverable except under certain circumstances. Rule of Civil Procedure 26(b)(3) provides that such material is only discoverable "upon a showing that the party seeking discovery has substantial need of the materials in the preparation of his case and that he is unable without undue hardship to obtain the substantial equivalent of the materials by other means." In addition, an attorney's work product is not discoverable[61]—by statute, trial preparation material that might otherwise be considered a public record is subject to the constraints of Rule of Civil Procedure 26(b)(3).[62] If litigation has not yet commenced, the custodian must, upon request, "provide a written justification for the assertion that the public record was prepared in anticipation of a legal proceeding."[63]

When the public records law does not apply, access to information about nontestifying experts is more limited. This issue was raised in *Mack v. Moore*,[64] a case in which a defendant asked the plaintiff to identify all

---

57. G.S. 132-1.

58. G.S. 132-1.1(a).

59. News & Observer Publishing Co. v. Poole, 330 N.C. 465, 481–82, 412 S.E.2d 7, 17 (1992).

60. G.S. 132-1.1(a).

61. G.S. 1A-1, Rule 26(b)(3).

62. G.S. 132-1.9(d).

63. G.S. 132-1.9(b).

64. 91 N.C. App. 478, 372 S.E.2d 314 (1988).

experts consulted but not intended to be called as experts at trial.[65] The court of appeals interpreted the rules as not requiring nontestifying experts to be disclosed as experts, but it noted that information about them as lay witnesses may be discoverable if they were involved in the matter being litigated. The court said, "If such an expert is not expected to testify, the identity of that expert is not discoverable. The identities of experts whose information is not acquired in anticipation of trial, such as actors or viewers of the occurrence that gave rise to the suit, are discoverable as ordinary non-expert witnesses."[66] The court did not address whether documents, such as reports, could be obtained if prepared in anticipation of litigation. North Carolina's rules of procedure do not have a rule similar to Federal Rule of Civil Procedure 26(b)(4)(B), which allows a party to discover opinions of experts not expected to testify upon a showing of exceptional circumstances under which it is impractical to discover this information by other means.[67]

2.7.2 Witnesses and Other Proof

A condemnor's preparation for an eminent domain proceeding ordinarily begins with obtaining the opinion of a state-certified appraiser subject to professional standards. This valuation expert should have experience valuing the type of property involved in the condemnation as well as knowledge of the current market. An expert may rely on information provided by others, including hearsay, if the information is "inherently reliable." As the North Carolina Court of Appeals noted, "An expert witness has wide latitude in gathering information and may base his opinion on evidence not otherwise admissible."[68] Of course the expert's opinion can be challenged on cross-examination based on the reliability of the information on which the expert relied, and an opinion can unravel if the underlying information is significantly flawed.

---

65. *Id.* at 479, 372 S.E.2d at 315.

66. *Id.* at 483, 372 S.E.2d at 317.

67. The comments to the North Carolina Rules of Civil Procedure note that the General Assembly deleted this provision during the legislative process but state that "[f]ailure to adopt this provision would not appear to foreclose such discovery on a proper showing under Rule 26(b)(3) [regarding trial preparation materials] or Rule 34 [regarding production of documents]." G.S. 1A-1, Rule 26 Comment to the 1975 Amendment, Section (b)(4), Note. As discussed in the text above, the court of appeals apparently has not so interpreted the North Carolina rule.

68. *In re* Lee, 69 N.C. App. 277, 287, 317 S.E.2d 75, 81 (1984).

Various experts, specialists, and professionals may be able to provide information or opinions helpful in determining real estate value. Valuation may entail consideration of site conditions, land use regulations, and other factors affecting the market value of a particular parcel. Potential witnesses include those experienced with the types of uses that are best for the subject property; land planners and engineers who can testify about best uses for the property; and brokers, developers, and others experienced in the relevant real estate markets. The trial court determines whether the individual has informative knowledge or perspective. As the North Carolina Supreme Court noted, "The competency of a witness to testify as an expert is a question primarily addressed to the sound discretion of the court, and his discretion is ordinarily conclusive."[69]

A commonly relied-upon indication of market value is the price paid for a similar property in the same neighborhood as the subject property. Such a price is the basis for the comparable sales approach. This information also can be relevant in the analysis of an expert opinion. As the North Carolina Supreme Court explained,

> "Dealing with direct testimony, it has been held that in the determination of fair market value of property taken in a condemnation case, evidence of price for which similar property has been sold in the vicinity may be admissible upon two separate theories and for two distinct purposes. First, such evidence may be admissible as substantive proof of the value of the condemned property, or secondly, it may be admissible, not as direct evidence of the value of the property under consideration, but in support of, and as background for, the opinion testified to by an expert as to the value of the property taken."[70]

Additionally, information about other properties may bear on the credibility of an expert opinion. As the court said, "A witness who expresses an opinion on property value may be cross-examined with respect to his *knowledge* of values of nearby properties for the limited purpose of testing the worthiness of his opinion, or challenging his credibility, even if those properties are not similar to that involved in the litigation. It is always the duty of the presiding

---

69. LaVecchia v. North Carolina Joint Stock Land Bank of Durham, 218 N.C. 35, 41, 9 S.E.2d 489, 492 (1940).

70. State Highway Comm'n v. Conrad, 263 N.C. 394, 399, 139 S.E.2d 553, 557–58 (1965) (quoting 5 NICHOLS ON EMINENT DOMAIN, 3d ed. § 21.3(2) at 437).

judge, however, to confine the nature and scope of this line of cross-examination to matters relevant to its limited impeachment purpose."[71]

Although owners are not likely to be experts in real estate valuation, they may have admissible information that could be useful for determining just compensation. The courts have recognized that owners may be in a position to provide such information. As the North Carolina Supreme Court noted,

> Unless it affirmatively appears that the owner does not know the market value of his property, it is generally held that he is competent to testify as to its value even though his knowledge on the subject would not qualify him as a witness were he not the owner. "He is deemed to have sufficient knowledge of the price paid, the rents or other income received, and the possibilities of the land for use, to have a reasonably good idea of what it is worth. The weight of his testimony is for the jury, and it is generally understood that the opinion of the owner is so far affected by bias that it amounts to little more than a definite statement of the maximum value of his contention."[72]

Therefore, "an owner is entitled to testify to the value of his own property 'unless it affirmatively appears' that the owner does not know the value."[73] Owners of neighboring property also may have helpful information if they can testify about the effect of condemnation on the value of their comparable properties, because such testimony could provide a measure of similar effect on the subject property.[74]

Local governments must base ad valorem property taxes on market valuations, and valuations for eminent domain purposes should be consistent with tax valuations. As the North Carolina Supreme Court has said, however, "Ad valorem tax records have historically been held incompetent as evidence of value of real property," because those who provided the valuation opinions

---

71. Duke Power Co. v. Winebarger, 300 N.C. 57, 63, 265 S.E.2d 227, 231 (1980) (emphasis in original) (citations omitted).

72. North Carolina State Highway Comm'n v. Helderman, 285 N.C. 645, 652, 207 S.E.2d 720, 725 (1974) (quoting 5 NICHOLS ON EMINENT DOMAIN § 18.4(2) (3d ed., 1969)).

73. Responsible Citizens in Opposition to the Flood Plain Ordinance v. City of Asheville, 308 N.C. 255, 271, 302 S.E.2d 204, 214 (1983).

74. *Id.*

are not witnesses in the eminent domain proceeding.[75] On the other hand, the North Carolina Court of Appeals has held that a tax valuation can be admissible as an admission of a party opponent when it is determined by the condemnor through its agents. [76]

To be relevant, a valuation must be sufficiently related in time to the eminent domain valuation date. There is no calibrated yardstick for determining whether any valuation is sufficiently timely. As the North Carolina Supreme Court pointed out, an assessment's relevance depends on "the nature of the property, its location and surrounding circumstances, and whether the evidence offered fairly points to its value at the time in question."[77]

2.8 Pleadings, Notices, and Other Litigation Requirements

As with all litigation, pleadings are important in eminent domain cases for several reasons. The statutes and common law set prerequisites for commencing and continuing litigation, which include the timing and minimum content of pleadings. As specified below, certain circumstances and facts must be alleged in eminent domain pleadings to establish a condemnor's authority to proceed, and a number of documents must be filed with the court or the register of deeds. When preparing and filing pleadings in an eminent domain case, the condemnor must consider that such pleadings may trigger vested rights that cannot be unraveled without the owner's cooperation or court involvement. In addition, the parties should keep the pleadings in mind throughout the litigation process. If relevant information is discovered or circumstances involving the project change, one or both parties should take appropriate action to amend the pleadings as soon as possible. Failure to comply with these requirements could result in delay, wasted expense, and even dismissal of the action.

Pleadings form part of the litigation record. Trial judges and appeals courts rely on pleadings for a glimpse of the nature of the dispute. Succinct,

---

75. R.R. v. Land Co., 137 N.C. 330, 332–33, 49 S.E. 350, 351 (1904).

76. Craven County v. Hall, 87 N.C. App. 256, 259–60, 360 S.E.2d 479, 480–81 (1987).

77. State Highway & Public Works Comm'n v. Hartley, 218 N.C. 438, 440, 11 S.E.2d 314, 315 (1940).

clear, and complete pleadings are important in helping a judge grasp the issues and make informed rulings. Claims, counterclaims, offsets, and many other matters must appropriately appear in the pleadings or they may be deemed to have been waived on appeal. Allegations in the pleadings about such matters as the purpose for the taking, related properties, and the nature of the interest to be acquired may become critically important to successful completion of an eminent domain case. Those involved in eminent domain proceedings must therefore consider carefully, at the outset, what matters are at stake, research the elements that comprise such matters, and include appropriate disclosures of these matters in appropriate pleadings filed at the appropriate time.

Chapter 40A contains a number of special procedural requirements that apply to local government eminent domain and inverse condemnation actions. In addition to the statutory requirements for such actions, those involved in eminent domain proceedings should consult local rules and other sources of information about a particular court's expectations and practices.

2.8.1 Notice of Intent to Enter Property

The statutes authorize condemnors to enter "any lands" to conduct investigations "as may be necessary or expedient in carrying out and performing . . . rights or duties" related to the eminent domain action for the purpose of surveying, making examinations, or conducting tests, including borings.[78] The statutes require that condemnors give at least thirty days' prior written notice to the owners and parties in possession before going onto the land.[79] The parties in possession entitled to notice would likely include those with recorded interests as well as parties about whom the condemnor has actual knowledge. The right of entry does not include a right to enter any structures.[80] By statute, owners are entitled to be reimbursed for any damage resulting from the entry, and, if the owner must seek court involvement for the reimbursement and the amount awarded is more than 25 percent greater than what the condemnor offered, the owner may recover attorneys' fees for the reimbursement action.[81]

---

78. G.S. 40A-11.
79. *Id.*
80. *Id.*
81. *Id.*

The following is a sample form of notice:

---

date

CERTIFIED MAIL
RETURN RECEIPT REQUESTED

NOTICE OF INTENT TO ENTER PROPERTY

TO: *name of owners and known possessors*
         addresses

    This letter is notice under Section 40A-11 of the North Carolina General Statutes that *authority that will institute the action* through its authorized representatives or agents intends to enter the property at *description of the property to be entered* to make surveys, borings, examinations, or appraisals as may be necessary or expedient in carrying out and performing its rights and duties in connection with its intent to institute an action to condemn by eminent domain the above-referenced property *or if other property is being acquired, a description of the property to be acquired*. The entry will occur on or after *a date not earlier than 30 days after the notice will have been given.* This work is in connection with *brief project description.* No structures will be entered without your prior express permission.

    Please contact *contact information for representative* if you have any questions or concerns.

signature of condemnor
condemnor's printed name

2.8.2 Notice of Action

G.S. 40A-40 requires that a public condemnor give to each owner of the subject property, whose name and address can be ascertained by reasonable diligence, written notice of the action at least thirty days before the complaint and declaration of taking will be filed. The notice must be sent by certified mail and is deemed complete upon proper mailing. The notice must include the following:

- A general description of the property to be taken
- The estimated just compensation

- The purpose for which the property is to be taken
- The date the condemnor intends to file the complaint

If the condemnation is a "quick take" under G.S. 40A-42, as to which title will vest when the complaint is filed, the notice must contain the aforementioned information as well as meet the following additional requirements:[82]

- It must be in at least twelve-point bold, legible type.
- The words "notice of condemnation" or similar must appear conspicuously in it.
- It must "contain a plain language summary of the owner's rights, including" "[t]he right to commence an action for injunctive relief" and "to answer the complaint after it has been filed."
- It must inform the owner "to consult with an attorney regarding the owner's rights."[83]

By statute, "[a]n owner is entitled to no relief because of any defect or inaccuracy in the notice unless the owner was actually prejudiced by the defect or inaccuracy, and the owner is otherwise entitled to relief under Rules 55(d) or 60(b) of the North Carolina Rules of Civil Procedure or other applicable law."[84] The North Carolina Court of Appeals has held that "[w]hile the statute does require that the notice state the 'purpose' of the action, it does not require the condemnor to state each and every intended 'use' of the condemned property."[85] The statute's intent seems to be satisfied when the owner is given enough information to understand the nature of the condemnor's project as contemplated at the time the notice is given. If the scope of the project changes materially after a notice has been given, the condemnor should consider giving further notice, even if technically it may not be required.

The following is a form of notice of action containing the minimum required information:

---

82. G.S. 40A-40(b).

83. *Id.*

84. G.S. 40A-40.

85. Scotland County v. Johnson, 131 N.C. App. 765, 769, 509 S.E.2d 213, 215 (1998).

date

CERTIFIED MAIL
RETURN RECEIPT REQUESTED

NOTICE OF ACTION

TO: *name(s) of owner(s) and others known to have*
rights in the property
addresses

This letter is a NOTICE OF ACTION under Chapter 40A-40 of the North Carolina General Statutes that *condemnor's name* intends to institute an action on *date complaint is intended to be filed* to condemn by eminent domain the property described below in which you have or claim an interest.

The purpose for which the property is being condemned is *brief project description*.

The property and interest being condemned is described as follows:

general description of the property to be taken

condemnor's name estimates that the amount of just compensation for the property condemned is *estimated compensation amount*.

If the condemnation is a "quick take" under G.S. 40A-42, as to which title will vest when the complaint is filed, notice providing the following information in at least twelve-point bold, legible type is required by G.S. 40A-40(b):

The condemnation action will be for a purpose as to which title to the property will immediately vest (with the right of exclusive possession) in *condemnor's name*, when the complaint is filed to institute the action to condemn, pursuant to North Carolina General Statutes 40A-42. You have a right to commence an action in superior court of the county in which the land is situated to request that the court grant injunctive relief to prevent title from vesting as described in the preceding sentence. You also have a right to answer the complaint after it has been filed. You are advised to consult with an attorney regarding your rights.

> *signature of condemnor*
> *condemnor's name and address*
> *and other contact information*

2.8.3 Complaint, Declaration of Taking, and Notice of Deposit

An action under Chapter 40A is commenced with the condemnor's pleading commonly entitled "Complaint, Declaration of Taking, and Notice of Deposit."[86] As with initial pleadings in other civil actions, the eminent domain complaint must include the essential allegations that, if proved or established, entitle the plaintiff to the requested relief. The condemnor must identify, include, or describe the following:

- A statement of the authority for the action and of the public use for which the property is taken
- The property to be acquired, and any other property affected, such as remaining property after part of a tract is taken
- All of the owners having an interest in the subject property, as broadly defined by G.S. 40A-2(5)
- A statement of the amount of estimated compensation
- The existence of liens or other encumbrances that can be ascertained
- Whether the owner may remove improvements or fixtures
- Notice that the required deposit has been made with the court
- A request for a determination of just compensation

The following form contains the minimum information required by statute:[87]

---

86. G.S. 40A-41.
87. *Id.*

NORTH CAROLINA	IN THE GENERAL COURT OF JUSTICE
county in which action filed COUNTY	SUPERIOR COURT DIVISION
	file number

condemnor's name,	COMPLAINT,
Plaintiff,	DECLARATION OF TAKING,
v.	AND NOTICE OF DEPOSIT
defendants' names,	
Defendants.	

1. Plaintiff, *condemnor's name* is a *type of organization* organized and existing under the laws of the State of North Carolina.

2. Plaintiff has the power of eminent domain vested in it by the General Assembly of North Carolina pursuant to *reference to the statute or session law granting the power of eminent domain for the condemnation*.

3. Plaintiff has determined that it is necessary and in the public interest to acquire the property that is the subject of this declaration of taking for the following project: *Provide description of the public use for which the property is taken.*

4. Those parties who are identified by name and address on Exhibit A hereto, are, so far as the same can by reasonable diligence be ascertained, the only persons who may have or claim to have an interest in the property that is the subject of this declaration of taking, and to plaintiff's knowledge and belief these persons are under no legal disability. *If any disabilities are known, so state. If the whereabouts of any owners are unknown, so state.*

5. The tract of land being taken is known as *identification of the tract*, more particularly described in Exhibit B attached hereto. *Attach Exhibit B with a description of the tract.*

If less than the entire tract is being taken, substitute:
5. The tract of land affected by the taking is known as *identification of the tract affected,* more particularly described in Exhibit B attached hereto. *Attach Exhibit B with a description of the tract or tracts affected.*

6. The property being taken is *statement of the nature of the interest taken, such as fee simple or sanitary sewer easement*, and is more particularly described in Exhibit B attached hereto. *Attach Exhibit B with a description of the area taken; this description may already be included in connection with paragraph 5 if the entire tract is being taken.*

7. In compliance with N.C.G.S. § 40A-40, at least 30 days prior to the filing of this action, notice of plaintiff's intent to institute this action was duly given to the owners whose names and addresses could be ascertained by reasonable diligence, and who are listed on Exhibit A hereto.

continued

continued

8. Plaintiff estimates the sum of $ *estimated compensation amount* to be just compensation for the taking of the property described in Exhibit B. Plaintiff hereby gives notice that it has this date deposited this sum to the use of the owner with the Superior Court of *county in which action filed* County. The defendants may apply to the Court for disbursement of such sum as full compensation, or as a credit against just compensation, as may be determined in this action.

9. Plaintiff will not permit the defendants to remove any timber, buildings, structures, permanent improvements or fixtures situated on or affixed to the property taken. *Or, describe the extent to which such property may be removed.*

10. The property that is the subject of this declaration of taking, insofar as the same can by reasonable diligence be ascertained, is subject only to such liens and encumbrances as follows: *List descriptions and register of deeds recording information for deeds of trust, assignments, easements, and other liens and encumbrances here.*

If the condemnation is of only a portion of a parcel, or only a portion of a building or other structure, and the remainder of the parcel or building is to be condemned, include a statement of the condemnor's determination regarding the required conditions set forth in G.S. 40A-7.

If the condemnation is a "quick take" under G.S. 40A-42, the following could be included: The property and area described herein are hereby declared to be taken and title thereto, together with the right of possession, shall vest in the plaintiff according to the provisions of G.S. 40A-42.

WHEREFORE, the plaintiff respectfully prays that the Court:

1. Determine the just compensation for the property interest taken in accordance with applicable law, and

2. Grant such other relief as the Court may deem appropriate.

date   *signature of condemnor's attorney*
                                         Attorney for *condemnor's name*
                                         attorney's name and address

---

Exhibit A

The names and addresses of those persons whom the condemnor is informed and believes may be, or claim to be, owners of the property so far as the same can by reasonable diligence be ascertained.

Exhibit B

Description of the entire tract or tracts of land affected by the taking, a statement of the property taken, and a description of the area taken.

2.8.4 Summons and Service

As with any civil proceeding, proper service of a summons is essential to commencing the proceeding properly and ultimately in securing a judgment that will bind all parties with interests in the matter.

2.8.4.1 Summons

G.S. 40A-41 requires service of the summons, with a copy of the complaint and notice of the deposit, in the manner prescribed by Rule of Civil Procedure 4. However, G.S. 40A-46 affords the defendants in a Chapter 40A public condemnation action 120 days from the date of service to file an answer. The judge may extend the deadline for another 30 days "for good cause shown and after notice to the condemnor."[88] Failure to file an answer by this deadline constitutes an admission that the amount deposited is just compensation and entitles the plaintiff to entry of final judgment and an order that the deposit be disbursed to the owner.[89]

The same form of summons used for a civil action is used for an eminent domain action. It must contain the title of the case (e.g., "Complaint, Declaration of Taking, and Notice of Deposit") and the court and county names and notify each defendant to answer within 120 days after service and that if the defendant fails to appear the plaintiff will apply to the court for the relief demanded in the complaint. The summons must also contain the plaintiff's attorney's name and address or, if there is no attorney, the plaintiff's address.[90]

2.8.4.2 Service

Acceptable methods of service are described in Rule of Civil Procedure 4.[91] Rule 4(j1) states that "[a] party that cannot with due diligence be served by personal delivery, registered or certified mail, or by a designated delivery service authorized pursuant to 26 U.S.C. § 7502(f)(2) may be served by publication." Publication service under Rule 4(j1) requires publication once a week for three successive weeks with a notice of service of publication in a newspaper that

---

88. G.S. 40A-46.
89. *Id.*
90. G.S. 1A-1, Rule 4(b).
91. G.S. 40A-41; G.S. 1A-4, Rule 4.

meets the requirements of G.S. 1-597 and G.S. 1-598. Such newspapers include daily or weekly newspapers of general circulation within the county or in the area where the party is believed to be located or, if no such location is known, in the county where the action is pending. If the party's mailing address is known or can be ascertained with reasonable diligence, a copy of the notice of service of process by publication must be mailed to the party upon or immediately prior to the first publication. Rule 4(j1) contains other specific requirements regarding the notice's content and method of publication. Proof of the publication is made by affidavit filed with the court, which should indicate the identity and last known addresses of those being served by publication and the reason for the use of this method.[92]

2.8.5 Memorandum of Action

A condemnor filing an eminent domain complaint must record a memorandum of action with the register of deeds in each county in which the land involved is located.[93] Condemnors want to ensure that the outcome of an eminent domain proceeding will bind any party acquiring an interest in the property after the action has been commenced. Purchasers and lenders take their interests subject to the rights of others whose interests were recorded, either pursuant to the real estate recording statutes[94] or the lis pendens statute for pending litigation.[95] The memorandum of action gives constructive public notice to potential purchasers and secured creditors about the pending eminent domain action. Accordingly, the memorandum should distinctly set forth the owners' names as they appear on the instruments from which the owners derive title, thus enabling the register to index the names in a manner in which the memorandum will be found. The memorandum should fully and accurately describe the affected property. The following form contains the minimum elements prescribed by statute:

---

92. G.S. 1A-1, Rule 4(j2).
93. G.S. 40A-43.
94. G.S. 47-18; G.S. 47-20; G.S. 47-27.
95. G.S. 1-118.

minimum 3-inch top margin for recording purposes

NORTH CAROLINA   IN THE GENERAL COURT OF JUSTICE
county in which action filed COUNTY   SUPERIOR COURT DIVISION
                                  file number

condemnor's name,   MEMORANDUM OF ACTION
    Plaintiff,
v.
defendants' names,
    Defendants.

PLEASE TAKE NOTICE:

1. On *date complaint filed*, plaintiff, *condemnor's name*, pursuant to the provisions of Chapter 40A of the North Carolina General Statutes, instituted the above-captioned civil action in the Superior Court of *county in which action filed* County to acquire by condemnation the real property interest hereinafter described.

2. The above-named defendants are the persons the plaintiff is informed and believes may have or claim to have an interest in the property.

3. The tract of land affected and being taken is known as *identification of the tract*, more particularly described as follows: *description of the tract*.

If less than the entire tract is being taken or other land is being affected, substitute the following two paragraphs for paragraph 3. above:
3. The tract of land affected by the taking is known as *identification of the tract affected,* more particularly described as follows: *description of the tract or tracts affected.*

4. The property being taken is *statement of the nature of the interest taken, such as fee simple or sanitary sewer easement*, and is more particularly described as follows: *description of the area taken. This description may already be included in connection with paragraph 2 if entire tract is being taken.*

date   *condemnor's name*
                                  By
                                  signature of condemnor's attorney
                                  attorney's address and telephone number

G.S. 1-116 provides that with respect to pending litigation "affecting title to real property," any person "desiring the benefit of constructive notice of pending litigation must file a separate, independent notice thereof," known as a lis pendens notice, with the superior court clerk of the county in which the action is pending and in which the real estate is located.[96] The contents of the notice are specified by G.S. 1-116, and the notice must be served on the other parties pursuant to G.S. 1-116.1. The notice is cross-indexed in the Record of Lis Pendens.[97] A recorded memorandum of action describing the subject property should suffice to give constructive notice of the eminent domain action to potential lienholders and purchasers, especially in an action in which title is deemed to have been transferred upon the filing of the complaint.[98] The lis pendens procedure provides greater assurance that there can be no question about sufficient notice.

2.8.6 Condemnor's Plat

Within ninety days from receipt of the answer but no sooner than six months after the complaint is filed, the condemnor must file with the court "a plat of the property taken and such additional area as may be necessary to properly determine the compensation," and a copy of the plat must be mailed to the parties or their attorneys.[99] Plats are important tools for commissioners, judges, and juries to use to visualize the issues they are being asked to consider. The plat depicts the extent to which the project has an impact on the owners' property and is an important illustration to use in determining the just compensation to be paid. Normally the plat's depiction "of the property taken and such additional area as may be necessary to determine the compensation" will reflect the "entire tract or tracts of the land affected by the taking" as specified in the complaint.

---

96. *See* Hughes v. North Carolina State Highway Comm'n, 275 N.C. 121, 127–28, 165 S.E.2d 321, 325 (1969) ("The statutory law as to lis pendens embodied in N. C. Gen. Stats. 1-116 *et seq.*, provides a definite method for giving constructive notice, so that a search of known records will convert it into actual notice. Since the application of this rule may work hardship in many instances, a strict compliance with its provisions is required").

97. G.S. 1-116; G.S. 1-117.

98. G.S. 40A-42 (specifying the purposes for which title vests upon filing of the complaint (the "quick take" procedure)); *see* section 2.5.1 (describing "quick take" purposes).

99. G.S. 40A-45(c).

Sometimes the plat is filed earlier than required, such as with the filing of the complaint. Although the statute does not require that a notice that the plat has been recorded be filed with the court, some practitioners file this notice with the plat.

2.8.7 Answer

Any person whose property has been taken by a condemnor may file an answer to the complaint. [100] Those served with a complaint have 120 days after the complaint was served to file an answer.[101] Failure to answer within the deadline is deemed to be an admission that the deposit is just compensation, and the judge is directed by statute to enter final judgment and to direct that the condemnor's deposit be disbursed to the owner.[102] The statutes also provide that "at any time prior to the entry of the final judgment the judge may, for good cause shown and after notice to the condemnor extend the time for filing answer for 30 days."[103]

An answer to a complaint filed in a Chapter 40A proceeding must contain at least the following:

- The names and addresses of the persons filing the answer, together with a statement as to their interests in the property taken
- Appropriate admissions or denials of the complaint's allegations
- Any affirmative defenses
- A request that just compensation be determined[104]

An owner wishing to have a jury determine compensation can make a demand for a jury trial in the answer.[105] In a counterclaim to a condemnation complaint, an owner may assert a claim of inverse condemnation if the owner maintains either that the condemnor took property other than what the condemnor seeks to acquire in the complaint or that property was taken before the action was filed.

---

100. G.S. 40A-45(a); G.S. 40A-46.

101. *Id.*

102. G.S. 40A-46.

103. *Id.*

104. G.S. 40A-45(a).

105. See section 2.3.2.2 regarding a right to a jury trial and the requirements for demanding a jury.

The statute provides that "[a] copy of the answer shall be served on the condemnor provided that failure to serve the answer shall not deprive the answer of its validity."[106]

2.8.8 Reply

Affirmative allegations in the defendant's answer are deemed denied without need for the condemnor to file a reply stating such denials.[107] The condemnor has thirty days after receipt of the answer to file a reply if the condemnor desires to do so.[108] A condemnor should file a reply if the owner's initial responsive pleading raises counterclaims to which the condemnor wishes to preserve affirmative defenses, such as a statute of limitations defense to an owner's counterclaim of inverse condemnation.

2.8.9 Deposit and Its Disbursement

When the complaint is filed, the condemnor must deposit with the clerk of court the amount estimated to be just compensation. The defendant owner may withdraw the deposit without prejudice to the parties' rights to challenge the amount of just compensation.[109] By statute, "[n]o notice to the condemnor of the hearing upon the application for disbursement of deposit shall be necessary."[110] If there are title issues regarding the defendant's ownership, the court must resolve the issues before the deposit can be withdrawn.[111] When there are competing claims to the deposit—as may occur if the property is subject to deeds of trust, tax assessments, or other rights to the property—the court is authorized to allocate the disbursement in a "just and equitable" manner.[112] Local governments may wish to allege in the complaint the existence of any unpaid property taxes, assessments, or other liens and request that the court first disburse the deposit to pay unpaid property taxes on the property to be acquired.

---

106. G.S. 40A-45(b).
107. *Id.*
108. *Id.*
109. G.S. 40A-44.
110. *Id.*
111. *Id.*; G.S. 40A-47.
112. G.S. 40A-44.

2.8.10 Appointment of Commissioners

As mentioned in section 2.3.2.1 above, within sixty days after the answer is filed either the condemnor or an owner may request the appointment of commissioners to determine compensation.[113] A condemnor may make the request in the complaint, the owner may make it in the answer, and either party may make it by separate motion before the deadline.[114] The clerk appoints the commissioners after any issues other than compensation have been resolved by the judge pursuant to G.S. 40A-47.

The statute provides that when a request has been appropriately made, the clerk appoints "three competent, disinterested persons residing in the county to serve as commissioners. The commissioners shall be sworn and shall go upon the land to appraise the compensation for the property taken and report their findings to the court within a time certain. Each commissioner shall be a person who has no right, title, or interest in or to the property being condemned, is not related within the third degree to the owner or to the spouse of the owner, is not an officer, employee, or agent of the condemnor, and is disinterested in the rights of the parties in every way."[115] The commissioners have considerable discretion to collect information and to develop their valuation analysis. By statute, "[t]he commissioners shall have the power to inspect the property, hold hearings, swear witnesses, and take evidence as they may, in their discretion, deem necessary, and shall file with the court a report of their determination of the damages sustained."[116] The practice for appointment of commissioners varies among the counties, and those involved in an eminent domain proceeding should consider making inquiries with the clerk regarding particular expectations.

The following is a sample motion for appointment of commissioners:

---

113. G.S. 40A-48(a).
114. *Id.*
115. *Id.*
116. G.S. 40A-48(b).

NORTH CAROLINA
county in which action filed COUNTY

IN THE GENERAL COURT OF JUSTICE
SUPERIOR COURT DIVISION
file number

condemnor's name,
  Plaintiff,
v.
defendants' names,
  Defendants.

MOTION FOR
APPOINTMENT OF
COMMISSIONERS

1. On *date complaint filed*, plaintiff, *condemnor's name*, pursuant to the provisions of Chapter 40A of the North Carolina General Statutes, instituted the above-captioned civil action in the Superior Court of *county in which action filed* County to acquire by condemnation the real property interest described in the Complaint, Declaration of Taking, and Notice of Deposit filed in this case.

2. All parties to this action are properly before the Court.

3. There are no issues in dispute concerning authorization to condemn, necessary parties, title to the land, or area taken, and the only disputed issue is the amount of just compensation.

4. G.S. 40A-48 provides that, upon motion of the plaintiff or defendant, the Clerk of the Superior Court shall appoint three Commissioners to go upon the property, appraise the damages resulting from the taking, and report the same to the Court within a time certain.

Consider addressing the identity of proposed commissioners and the manner in which they will be compensated.

WHEREFORE, plaintiff, *condemnor's name*, respectfully moves that the Clerk of the Superior Court appoint three disinterested persons who are residents of this county to exercise their powers and duties under G.S. 40A-48 and appraise the compensation for the property taken.

date

signature of condemnor's attorney
Attorney for *condemnor's name*
attorney's name and address

CERTIFICATE OF SERVICE

I, the undersigned attorney for *party status and name*, certify that I have served a copy of the foregoing Motion by depositing a copy thereof, postage pre-paid, in the United States mail, to *name of each person served* at *service address of each person served*.

date

signature of condemnor's attorney
Attorney for *condemnor's name*
attorney's name and address

The following is a sample form of court order appointing the commissioners, which may appropriately be supplemented with any necessary direction about payment of the commissioners' compensation:

NORTH CAROLINA
county in which action filed COUNTY

IN THE GENERAL COURT OF JUSTICE
SUPERIOR COURT DIVISION
file number

condemnor's name,
    Plaintiff,

v.

defendants' names,
    Defendants.

BEFORE THE CLERK

ORDER APPOINTING
COMMISSIONERS

THIS CAUSE, coming on to be heard and being heard before the Honorable *clerk's name*, Clerk of Superior Court, on *hearing date*, and it appearing to the Court from the pleadings filed that the only disputed issue to be determined is the amount of compensation for the taking; and it further appearing that, pursuant to G.S. 40A-48(a), *party status and name of party moving for appointment* has by Answer/Motion filed on *date of motion* requested that Commissioners be appointed to appraise the damage to the defendant's property sustained by reason of this action.

NOW, THEREFORE, IT IS ORDERED that *commissioners' names*, all of whom are disinterested and competent residents of this County where the premises are to be appraised, are hereby appointed as Commissioners to review the premises referred to in the Complaint and, in their discretion, to hold hearings, swear witnesses, and take evidence as they may deem necessary. After such proceedings are completed, the Commissioners shall ascertain and determine the compensation that ought justly to be paid by the plaintiff to the defendants by reason of the condemnation, in accordance with Article 4, Chapter 40A of the North Carolina General Statutes. The Commissioners shall report their determination to the Court no later than *a specific date or a number of days within which the report is to be filed.*

IT IS FURTHER ORDERED that the Commissioners meet at the office of the Clerk of Superior Court at *time and date for first meeting and oath*, to subscribe their oath and proceed with the discharge of their duties.

date

signature of clerk
Clerk of Superior Court

2.8.11 Commissioners' Report

G.S. 40A-48(c) contains a form for the commissioners' report and states that the report must substantially comply with this form. However, the statutory form contains language that, if unmodified, incorrectly indicates that an owner receives both a sum for property taken and compensation for land remaining after the taking. As described in section 3.4 below, when a local public condemnor acquires a portion of property under Chapter 40A, the owner is entitled to the greater of either the value of the property taken or the diminished value to the remainder. [117] The following form is a modification of the statutory form to reflect this rule:

TO THE SUPERIOR COURT OF *county in which filed* COUNTY

We, *commissioners' names*, Commissioners appointed by the Court to assess the compensation to be awarded to *property owners' names*, the owner(s) of property interest in certain land lying in *county name* County, North Carolina, which has been taken by the *condemnor's name*, (condemnor), for public purposes, do hereby certify that we convened, and, having first been duly sworn, visited the premises, and took such evidence as was presented to us, and after taking into full consideration the quality and quantity of the land and all other facts which reasonably affect its fair market value at the time of the taking, we have determined the fair market value of the property taken to be the sum of $ *amount*.

If there is a taking of less than the entire tract, add:
and the amount by which the fair market value of the entire tract immediately before the taking exceeds the fair market value of the remainder immediately after the taking is the sum of $ *amount*.

GIVEN under our hands, this the *date* day of *month*, *year*.

commissioner's signature (SEAL)

commissioner's signature (SEAL)

commissioner's signature (SEAL)

---

117. G.S. 40A-64.

The clerk sends a copy of the commissioners' report to the parties or their counsel of record by certified or registered mail.[118]

2.8.12 Notice of Appeal from Commissioners' Report

The parties have thirty days after the commissioners' report is mailed to file exceptions to the report and to demand a jury trial in the superior court on the issue of compensation.[119] A party must file exceptions to the commissioners' report to be able to appeal the commissioners' decision.[120] The parties may jointly waive a jury trial and have the issue decided by the judge.[121] Neither the commissioners' report nor the condemnor's estimate of compensation as reflected by the deposit may be used as evidence in the trial of the amount of compensation.[122]

The statutes require the court to make a ruling about whether the commissioners' award is just compensation regardless of whether a party contests the award.[123] A court is unlikely to reject or even scrutinize a commissioners' award if the parties do not challenge it. By statute, if the court decides in its discretion that the commissioners' award is not just compensation, the matter is transferred to the civil docket for trial by jury.[124]

The following is a form that could be used as a notice of appeal by a party who objects to the commissioners' report. The notice must be filed within thirty days after the report was mailed.

---

118. G.S. 40A-48(d).
119. *Id.*
120. City of Raleigh v. Martin, 59 N.C. App. 627, 297 S.E. 2d 916 (1982).
121. G.S. 40A-48(d).
122. *Id.*
123. *Id.*
124. *Id.*

NORTH CAROLINA IN THE GENERAL COURT OF JUSTICE
county in which action filed COUNTY SUPERIOR COURT DIVISION
file number

condemnor's name, *PLAINTIFF'S/DEFENDANT'S*
  Plaintiff, EXCEPTION TO
v. COMMISSIONERS' AWARD AND
defendants' names, DEMAND FOR JURY TRIAL
  Defendants.

  appellant's party status and name, pursuant to G.S. 40A-48 hereby excepts from the Report of the Commissioners of Appraisal filed in this matter on *date of commissioners' report*, and gives Notice of Appeal for a trial de novo on the issue of just compensation.

date   *signature of condemnor's attorney*
     Attorney for *condemnor's name*
     attorney's name and address

CERTIFICATE OF SERVICE

  I, the undersigned attorney for *party status and name*, certify that I have served a copy of the foregoing by depositing a copy thereof, postage prepaid, in the United States mail, to *name of each person served* at *service address of each person served*.

date   *signature of condemnor's attorney*
     Attorney for *condemnor's name*
     attorney's name and address

2.9 Abandonment of Project during Proceeding

A condemnor who has begun an eminent domain proceeding may have great difficulty abandoning the acquisition. Title may have already changed hands, as occurs with the "quick take" process common in local government condemnations as described in section 2.5.1 above. The owner may have already withdrawn compensation from the deposit. Among other things, the owner's cooperation and court involvement may be necessary. G.S. 40A-8 contains special cost allocation rules applicable in the rare instance in which a condemnor abandons an eminent domain action after filing the complaint.

G.S. 40A-8 specifies that the court shall award each owner of the subject property "a sum that, in the opinion of the court based upon its findings of fact, will reimburse the owner for: his reasonable costs; disbursements; expenses (including reasonable attorney, appraisal, and engineering fees); and, any loss suffered by the owner because he was unable to transfer title to the property from the date of the filing of the complaint under G.S. 40A-41."[125] The statute refers to "reasonable costs." The North Carolina Supreme Court, applying a similar statute governing an award of costs in a Department of Transportation condemnation, held that the reasonableness requirement gives the court discretion to determine whether to order requested components of the awards, including attorneys' fees.[126]

As described in section 2.12 below, if a condemnor acquires title to property acquired by eminent domain and later determines that it is not needed for the purpose for which it was acquired, G.S. 40A-70 authorizes the condemnor to reconvey the property to the owner on certain terms and conditions.

2.10 Judgment and Payment of Compensation

The judgment is an important record in an eminent domain proceeding. It is recorded with the register of deeds and becomes a link in the chain of title for the acquired real property. The condemnor should prepare the property description with the same care as would be exercised with a deed. A certified copy of the judgment must be recorded with the register of deeds in each county in which any part of the real estate lies.[127] The parties also will need to consider whether recitations should be included to make a record of issues that were heard and how they were resolved. Any party expecting to appeal should ensure that the judgment and any opinions reflect that pertinent issues were raised at the appropriate time and therefore have been preserved for appeal.

The parties may be able to reach an agreement on the amount of compensation at any time during an eminent domain proceeding, including after the

---

125. G.S. 40A-8(b).

126. Lea Co. v. North Carolina Bd. of Transp., 323 N.C. 691, 694, 374 S.E.2d 868, 870–71 (1989) (applying G.S. 136-199).

127. G.S. 40A-54.

commissioners issue their report or a jury renders its verdict. The parties could structure their agreement as a conventional negotiated exchange of a deed for payment, reflected in the public records as such, rather than a court order resulting from litigation. Or they may prefer to resolve the case by consent judgment, for the sake of procedural simplicity, and to address any unresolved questions or claims. In this case the parties should request that the court enter a consent judgment, which would be recorded with the register of deeds to make a record of the title transfer. The judgment should address all issues regarding satisfaction of the procedural requirements, ownership, and compensation. All parties would join in the request for entry of the judgment, and the court's order should reflect that consent. Customarily the parties prepare a proposed consent order, endorse it, and present it to the court with a request that it be approved. A form of consent judgment appears below. As with all forms in this book, the proposed judgment, and the parties' request that the court enter it, should be tailored to the particular issues and circumstances of each case.

NORTH CAROLINA *county in which action filed* COUNTY	IN THE GENERAL COURT OF JUSTICE SUPERIOR COURT DIVISION *file number*

condemnor's name,
    Plaintiff,
v.
defendants' names,
    Defendants.
	CONSENT JUDGMENT

This case being heard before the Honorable *judge's name*, Superior Court Judge Presiding, upon a joint motion by the parties, and it further appearing to the Court and the Court finding as fact that:

1. The above-entitled civil action was instituted in this Court on *date of complaint*, by the issuance of summons and the filing of a Complaint, Declaration of Taking, and Notice of Deposit along with the deposit into the Court of $ *deposit amount*, the sum estimated by the plaintiff to be just compensation for the taking of the defendants' property.

2. Summons, together with a copy of the Complaint, Declaration, and Notice, were duly served upon the defendants, who represent all the parties having or claiming to have an interest in the property.

3. There are no issues in dispute concerning authorization to condemn, necessary parties, title to the land, or area taken, and the only unresolved matter is the amount of just compensation for the property taken.

4. All parties have agreed to final disposition of this matter on the terms described in this Consent Judgment.

continued

continued

5. *terms of the parties' agreement, including transfer of title and payment of just compensation*.

WHEREUPON, THE COURT CONCLUDES AS A MATTER OF LAW THAT:

1. The plaintiff is entitled to acquire by eminent domain the hereinafter described property of the defendants.

2. The sum of $ *amount* is just compensation for the property acquired by the plaintiff by eminent domain as hereinafter described.

3. These proceedings as appears from the pleadings are regular in all respects, and no reason exists for not entering final judgment.

NOW, THEREFORE, IT IS ADJUDGED AND ORDERED that:

1. Final judgment is hereby entered.

2. Plaintiff, *condemnor's name*, on *complaint date*, by the filing of a Complaint, Declaration of Taking, and Notice of Deposit, has condemned and is permanently vested with, the property, interest or estate, as of the date of the complaint, said property described as follows:

full description of the property interest and area condemned

If the condemnation was not a "quick take" under G.S. 40A-42, the introductory phrase in the preceding paragraph 2 should be altered to state when title vested or vests.

3. The amount of just compensation for the property to be paid to the owner is $ *amount*.

4. *Consider specifying agreement on costs and interest.*

5. The deposit shall be disbursed by the Clerk of Court as follows:

description of how the deposit is to be disbursed, including instructions for payment of any taxes and assessments owed on the property taken; also any additional instructions necessary for payment of just compensation, interest, and any awarded costs

6. Plaintiff shall cause to be recorded a copy of this Consent Judgment with the register of deeds of any county in which the subject premises are located.

date

judge's signature

SUPERIOR COURT JUDGE PRESIDING

The status of any real estate taxes and assessments on the condemned property should also be taken into consideration. To the extent that such taxes and assessments are unpaid from prior tax years, the condemnor may request that the deposit be disbursed to pay those amounts. Although the statute does not specifically provide that the deposit should be applied to unpaid taxes, the value of the property logically is affected by amounts that any prospective purchaser would have to satisfy with respect to the property.[128] A lien attaches on January 1 for the next tax year and taxes normally are prorated based on a calendar year.[129] The owner is entitled to reimbursement of taxes allocable to the period after title vests in the condemnor. When only part of the owner's land is acquired, including in the case of easements, any proration of property taxes would also involve proration by area and property interest.

The following is a sample form that could be used to move for entry of judgment based on the commissioners' award, if the moving party is satisfied with the award and does not wish to demand a trial de novo by a jury on the issue of compensation.

NORTH CAROLINA	IN THE GENERAL COURT OF JUSTICE
county in which action filed COUNTY	SUPERIOR COURT DIVISION
	file number
condemnor's name,	*PLAINTIFF'S/DEFENDANT'S*
Plaintiff,	MOTION FOR JUDGMENT
v.	ON COMMISSIONERS' AWARD
defendants' names,	
Defendants.	

1. The above-entitled civil action was instituted in this Court on *date of complaint*, by the issuance of Summons and the filing of a Complaint, Declaration of Taking, and Notice of Deposit, along with the deposit into the Court of $ *deposit amount*, the sum estimated by the plaintiff to be just compensation for the taking of the property of the defendants.

continued

---

128. G.S. 105-385(a) requires that in a judicial sale the judgment is to order taxes to be paid from the proceeds and allocated between the parties, and in a government purchase G.S. 105-385(c) requires that the unpaid taxes be deducted from the purchase price. Although an eminent domain acquisition is not mentioned in the statute, at least by analogy the unpaid taxes allocable to the owner's period of ownership should be borne by the owner.

129. *See* G.S. 39-60 (calendar year prorations for conveyances unless the contract provides otherwise).

continued

2. Summons, together with a copy of the Complaint, Declaration, and Notice, were duly served upon the defendants, who represent all the parties having or claiming to have an interest in the property.

3. There are no issues in dispute concerning authorization to condemn, necessary parties, title to the land, or area taken, and the only unresolved matter is the amount of just compensation for the property taken.

4. Commissioners were duly appointed to appraise and report the damages resulting from the taking, and the Commissioners filed their report on *date of Commissioners' Report*, a copy of which was duly mailed by the Clerk to each of the parties on *date report was mailed*.

5. *description of disposition of deposit and any additional sums deposited with the Clerk*

6. More than thirty days have elapsed since the mailing of the Commissioners' Report to the defendants, and no exceptions to the report have been filed, or any extension of time to file exceptions granted.

7. Pursuant to G.S. 40A-48, if no exception to the Commissioners' Report is filed within the time prescribed, final judgment shall be entered upon a determination by the Court that the Commissioners' Report, plus interest computed in accordance with G.S. 40A-53, awards to the property owners just compensation.

8. The legal description of the property condemned is as follows:

full description of the property interest and area condemned

Here include any requests with respect to an award of costs.

WHEREFORE, *party status and name of moving party* respectfully moves the Court to:

1. Find and determine that the Commissioners' Report, plus statutory interest, awards to the property owners just compensation.

2. Order that the sum deposited with the court by the plaintiff in the amount of the Commissioners' Award, including interest, be disbursed to the defendants, consistent with the Commissioners' Report, as follows:

continued

continued

> *description of how the deposit is to be disbursed, including instructions for payment*
> *of any taxes and assessments owed on the property taken; also any additional*
> *information necessary for the court to order payment of just compensation, interest,*
> *and costs*
>
> 3. Declare that the plaintiff has condemned, and is permanently vested with,
> the property, interest, or estate, as of the date of the complaint.
> *If the condemnation was not a "quick take" under G.S. 40A-42 as to which title*
> *vested when the complaint was filed, alter this paragraph to state when title vested*
> *or vests.*
>
> 4. Enter final judgment in this matter.
>
> *date*   *signature of condemnor's attorney*
>   Attorney for *condemnor's name*
>   *attorney's name and address*
>
> ### CERTIFICATE OF SERVICE
>
> I, the undersigned attorney for *party status and name*, certify that I have
> served a copy of the foregoing Motion by depositing a copy thereof, postage pre-
> paid, in the United States mail, to *name of each person served* at *service address of*
> *each person served*.
>
> *date*   *signature of condemnor's attorney*
>   Attorney for *condemnor's name*
>   *attorney's name and address*

The motion should provide the court with sufficient information to order disbursement of any remaining deposit and payment of any necessary additional
amounts, statutory interest, and costs. The moving party should consider
including a proposed judgment for the court's use, and local rules or practice
may require it. Modified versions of this form could be used for motions for
judgment based on decisions made by a jury, the court, or by consent, rather
than by commissioners.

The following is a basic form for a judgment on a commissioners' award:

NORTH CAROLINA   IN THE GENERAL COURT OF JUSTICE
county in which action filed COUNTY SUPERIOR COURT DIVISION
                    file number

condemnor's name,   FINAL JUDGMENT
  Plaintiff,   ON COMMISSIONERS' AWARD
v.
defendants' names,
  Defendants.

This case being heard before the Honorable *judge's name*, Superior Court Judge Presiding, upon Motion by Plaintiff for Final Judgment pursuant to G.S. 40A-48, and it further appearing to the Court and the Court finding as fact that:

1. The above-entitled civil action was instituted in this Court on *date of complaint*, by the issuance of summons and the filing of a Complaint, Declaration of Taking, and Notice of Deposit along with the deposit into the Court of $ *deposit amount*, the sum estimated by the plaintiff to be just compensation for the taking of the defendants' property.

2. Summons, together with a copy of the Complaint, Declaration, and Notice, were duly served upon the defendants, who represent all the parties having or claiming to have an interest in the property.

3. There are no issues in dispute concerning authorization to condemn, necessary parties, title to the land, or area taken, and the only unresolved matter is the amount of just compensation for the property taken.

4. Commissioners were duly appointed to appraise and report the damages resulting from the taking, and the commissioners filed their Report on *date of Commissioners' Report*, a copy of which was duly mailed by the Clerk to each of the parties on *date report was mailed*.

5. *description of disposition of deposit and any additional sums deposited with the Clerk*

6. More than thirty days have elapsed since the mailing of the Commissioners' Report to the defendants, and no exceptions to the report have been filed, or any extension of time to file exceptions granted.

7. Pursuant to G.S. 40A-48, if no exception to the Commissioners' Report is filed within the time prescribed, final judgment shall be entered upon a determination by the Court that the Commissioners' Report, plus interest computed in accordance with G.S. 40A-53, awards to the property owners just compensation.

continued

continued

WHEREUPON, THE COURT CONCLUDES AS A MATTER OF LAW
THAT:

    1. No exceptions having been filed to the Commissioners' Report within
thirty days from the mailing of the report to the parties by the Clerk, final
judgment is to be entered in this matter.

    2. These proceedings as appears from the pleadings are regular in all
respects, and no reason exists for not entering final judgment.

NOW, THEREFORE, IT IS ADJUDGED AND ORDERED that:

    1. Final judgment is hereby entered.

    2. Plaintiff, *condemnor's name,* on *complaint date,* by the filing of a Com-
plaint, Declaration of Taking, and Notice of Deposit, has condemned and is
permanently vested with, the property, interest or estate, as of the date of the
complaint, said property described as follows:

    full description of the property interest and area condemned

*If the condemnation was not a "quick take" under G.S. 40A-42, the introductory
phrase in the preceding paragraph 2 should be altered to state when title vested or
vests.*

    3. The amount of just compensation for the property to be paid to the
owner is $ *amount,* to which shall be added interest at the rate as specified in
G.S. 40A-53.

    4. *order with respect to whether any costs are awarded as allowed by
G.S. 40A-8*

    5. The deposit shall be disbursed by the Clerk of Court as follows:

*description of how the deposit is to be disbursed, including instructions for payment of any
taxes and assessments owed on the property taken; also any additional instructions necessary for payment of just compensation, interest, and any awarded costs*

    6. Plaintiff shall cause to be recorded a copy of this Judgment with the regis-
ter of deeds of any county in which the subject premises are located.

date
judge's signature
SUPERIOR COURT JUDGE PRESIDING

2.11   Costs and Attorneys' Fees

In an ordinary eminent domain case, the court has the discretion to order that a condemnor reimburse the owner for costs paid for appraisers, engineers, and plats.[130] Courts typically do order such reimbursement in eminent domain cases. A separate statute authorizes courts to assess court costs to the condemnors.[131] In the unusual case in which the action concludes with a final judgment that the condemnor was not authorized to condemn the property, or the condemnor abandons the acquisition, the owner also may be entitled to recover attorneys' fees and other losses and expenses as described in section 2.9 above.[132]

When the owner, rather than the condemnor, has brought the claim for compensation for inverse condemnation as discussed in Chapter 4, the statute requires that the court include as a part of the judgment a sum that, in the court's opinion based on findings of fact, will reimburse the owner for reasonable costs, disbursements, attorneys' fees, appraisal and engineering fees, and losses determined to have been caused by inability to transfer the property.[133]

2.12   Return of Condemned Property

Chapter 40A allows a condemnor to reconvey property taken by eminent domain to the former owner if the condemnor determines that it is not needed for the purpose for which it was condemned.[134] This authority enables a condemnor to transfer the property to the former owner without having to follow the usual procedures for local government sale of property. When an entire parcel was taken, the former owner may reacquire it for the amount paid to the former owner in the condemnation, plus the cost of any improvements and interest at the legal rate.[135] If less than an entire parcel was taken, the former owner may only reacquire it pursuant to this statute if the former

---

130. G.S. 40A-8(a).
131. G.S. 40A-13.
132. G.S. 40A-8(b).
133. G.S. 40A-8(c).
134. G.S. 40A-70.
135. *Id.*

owner still owns the remainder.[136] The condemnor must specify a date for reconveyance and payment, which must be at least thirty days after the former owner has been given written notice of this opportunity for repurchase and of the condemnor's designated date for reconveyance.[137]

2.13 Inverse Condemnation Procedure

As discussed in Chapter 4, an owner who claims that a government entity has taken property without first acquiring it through an eminent domain procedure may have a claim to compensation for inverse condemnation. The procedure for an owner to commence an inverse condemnation action for compensation under Chapter 40A is specified in G.S. 40A-51. Chapter 40A prescribes a time limit for the owner to bring such an action: "The action may be initiated within 24 months of the date of the taking of the affected property or the completion of the project involving the taking, whichever shall occur later."[138] The North Carolina Supreme Court has explained that this time constraint is meant to "provide plaintiffs adequate opportunity to discover damage."[139] The action is commenced with a complaint filed in superior court, which must contain the following:

- The names and places of residence of all persons who are, or claim to be, owners of the property, so far as these can by reasonable diligence be ascertained; a statement of the legal disabilities of any of these persons must also be included
- A statement as to any encumbrances on the property
- The particular facts that constitute the taking and the date that the facts allegedly occurred
- A description of the property taken[140]

---

136. *Id.*

137. *Id.*

138. G.S. 40A-51(a).

139. McAdoo v. City of Greensboro, 91 N.C App. 570, 572, 372 S.E.2d 742, 743–44 (1988).

140. G.S. 40A-51(a).

A summons with a copy of the complaint must be served on the alleged condemnor. By statute, the allegations are deemed denied, but the alleged condemnor may file an answer within sixty days of service.[141] If the condemnor admits the taking, the estimated amount of compensation must be deposited with the court when the answer is filed, with notice of the deposit given to the owner.[142] The procedure for disbursement of the deposit is the same as when a condemnor initiates the action, as described in section 2.8.9 above. [143] If the taking is admitted, the condemnor must file a plat of the property taken within ninety days after the answer is filed.[144] The procedure is otherwise the same as described above for an eminent domain action.[145]

An owner bringing an action under Chapter 40A for inverse condemnation must, when filing the complaint, also file a memorandum of action with the register of deeds in every county in which the property is located.[146] By statute, the memorandum must contain the following:

- The names of the persons the owner is informed and believes to be or claim to be owners of the property
- A description of the entire tract or tracts affected by the alleged taking sufficient for the identification of those tracts
- A statement of the property allegedly taken
- The date on which the owner alleges the taking occurred, the date on which said action was instituted, the county in which it was instituted, and any other references necessary for the identification of the action[147]

The law of inverse condemnation in North Carolina is discussed in Chapter 4.

---

141. *Id.*
142. *Id.*
143. *Id.*
144. *Id.*
145. *Id.*
146. G.S. 40A-51(b).
147. *Id.*

3   Just Compensation

3.1   **Fair Market Value   97**

3.2   **Valuation Methods   99**

    3.2.1   Market Comparison Approach   99

    3.2.2   Income Approach   100

    3.2.3   Cost Approach   100

3.3   **Date as to Which Value Is Measured   101**

3.4   **Valuation of Partial Takings   102**

3.5   **Effect of Public Improvements   102**

    3.5.1   Property Taken   103

    3.5.2   Remaining Property   104

3.6   **Affected Property   107**

    3.6.1   Ownership Unity   107

    3.6.2   Physical Unity   108

    3.6.3   Use Unity   109

3.7   **Several Interests and Extraction Rights   109**

3.8   **Loss of Business Income   111**

3.9   **Easements   113**

3.10   **Leases   115**

3.11   **Life Estates   116**

3.12   **Real Estate Liens   117**

3.13   **Relocation Assistance   118**

3.14   **Interest   120**

3.1   Fair Market Value

The United States and North Carolina constitutions require that the government pay just compensation to owners from whom private property is taken. The North Carolina Supreme Court stated this principle as follows: "We recognize the fundamental right to just compensation as so grounded in natural law and justice that it is part of the fundamental law of this State, and imposes upon a governmental agency taking private property for public use a correlative duty to make just compensation to the owner of the property taken. This principle is considered in North Carolina as an integral part of 'the law of the land' within the meaning of Article I, Section 19 of our State Constitution."[1] While the right to payment of just compensation is clear, the required amount of compensation can be the subject of considerable disagreement.

In 1905 the North Carolina Supreme Court encapsulated the essence of determining just compensation with the following explanation:[2]

> Certainly where by compulsory process and for the public good the State invades and takes the property of its citizens, in the exercise of its highest prerogative in respect to property, it should pay to him *full compensation*. The highest authorities are to that effect. "The market value of property is the price which it will bring when it is offered for sale by one who desires but is not obliged to sell it, and is bought by one who is under no necessity of having it. In estimating its value all the capabilities of the property and all the uses to which it may be applied or for which it is adapted may be considered and not merely the condition it is in at the time and the use to which it is then applied by the owner."[3]

The statutes governing local government condemnations, Chapter 40A, reflect the courts' interpretation of the constitutionally required just compensation. Section 40A-64 states that "the measure of compensation for a taking of property is its fair market value," except for an alternative measure

---

1. Long v. City of Charlotte, 306 N.C. 187, 196, 293 S.E.2d 101, 107–8 (1982).

2. Brown v. W.T. Weaver Power Co., 140 N.C. 333, 52 S.E. 954 (1905).

3. *Id.* at 341–42, 52 S.E. at 957 (quoting JOHN LEWIS, EMINENT DOMAIN § 478) (emphasis in original).

available to owners when only part of a tract is acquired, as described in section 3.4 below. Fair market value for just compensation purposes is based on the acquired property's potential "highest and best use," not just its current or its currently contemplated use. As the North Carolina Supreme Court explained, "In determining the value of land appropriated for public purposes, the same considerations are to be regarded as in a sale of property between private parties. The inquiry in such cases must be, what is the property worth in the market, viewed not merely with reference to the uses to which it is at the time applied, but with reference to the uses to which it is plainly adapted—that is to say, what is it worth from its availability for valuable uses?"[4] For example, property used for an orphanage within an urban area may have little marketability for such a limited but important purpose, but a much higher monetary value for commercial development, and this higher value is the measure of compensation.[5] Fair market value is based on a hypothetical willing buyer and a hypothetical informed purchaser considering such highest and best uses.[6]

A parcel's capacity for subdivision and development is a consideration for determining its market value. Appraisers take parcel size and physical characteristics into account to determine what a potential purchaser would pay. One factor to be considered in this analysis is the likelihood of obtaining required local land use approvals. If approvals are unlikely because of the property's characteristics, the value would appropriately be less than if the approvals have been obtained. The North Carolina Court of Appeals has said that "[i]f an owner has taken steps prior to the date of taking to adapt his land for future uses, the future uses to which the land is adapted are admissible."[7] For example, if a development plan has received regulatory approvals and roads have been constructed, the property likely would be valued as subdivided lots.[8]

---

4. Carolina–Tennessee Power Co. v. Hiawassee River Power Co., 186 N.C. 179, 183–84, 119 S.E. 213, 215 (1923) (quoting Boom Co. v. Patterson, 98 U.S. 403, 407–8 (1879)).

5. Gallimore v. State Highway & Public Works Comm'n, 241 N.C. 350, 355–56, 85 S.E.2d 392, 397 (1955).

6. *Id.* at 356, 85 S.E.2d at 397 ("[T]he application of our concept of fair market value does not depend upon the actual availability of one or more prospective purchasers, but assumes the existence of a buyer who is ready, able and willing to buy but under no necessity to do so").

7. City of Wilson v. Hawley, 156 N.C. App. 609, 613, 577 S.E.2d 161, 164 (2003).

8. Town of Hillsborough v. Crabtree, 143 N.C. App. 707, 547 S.E.2d 139 (2001).

On the other hand, valuations based on speculative uses or on unreasonable optimism about regulatory approvals would likely not be considered.

3.2 Valuation Methods

Statutes and case law require that compensation be based on fair market value. The North Carolina Supreme Court has identified three acceptable methods of real estate valuation for determining the fair market value of property for the purpose of eminent domain compensation. They are the market comparison approach, the income approach, and the cost approach.[9] The appropriateness of any particular approach depends on the nature of the property and the availability of market information. In some cases more than one approach is used, and the fact finder considers each result to determine fair market value. The compensation value can be based on one of the approaches or a reconciliation of all three, or it can be a different figure based on information from all three.

3.2.1 Market Comparison Approach

The North Carolina Supreme Court described the market comparison approach as "consideration of the rentals and prices obtained from the lease or sale of comparable properties reasonably related in respect of location and time."[10] Market comparison is the most common valuation method for real estate, and it is the usual approach for appraisal of residential properties. Appraisers will identify neighborhoods with properties similar to the subject parcel, research recent sales information, and make adjustments for differences in lot and building size and characteristics. The North Carolina Supreme Court described the extent to which comparisons can be made in *Barnes v. North Carolina State Highway Commission*[11] as follows: "Actually no two parcels of land are exactly alike. Only such parcels may be compared where the dissimilarities are reduced to a minimum and allowance is made for such dissimilarities. . . . It is within the sound discretion of the trial judge to determine whether there is sufficient similarity to render the evidence of

---

9. Redevelopment Comm'n of High Point v. Denny Roll & Panel Co., 273 N.C. 368, 370, 159 S.E.2d 861, 863 (1968).
10. *Id.* at 371, 159 S.E.2d at 863.
11. 250 N.C. 378, 109 S.E.2d 219 (1959).

sale admissible. It is the better practice for the judge to hear evidence in the absence of the jury as a basis for determining admissibility."[12] The parties often disagree about these comparisons.

3.2.2 Income Approach

The income approach reflects the reality that income-producing property, such as a shopping center, is purchased for investment, and the amount a purchaser will pay for the property reflects anticipated returns based on the property's characteristics and the market for such properties. The appraiser using an income approach calculates anticipated income using information about market rents, vacancy rates, maintenance and operating costs, and sometimes other factors and converts the anticipated income stream to a value using an "income rate" or "discount rate" intended to reflect the present value of the anticipated income stream.[13] Although the income approach is a well-recognized valuation method based on realistic investor expectations,[14] it is not as readily understood as the comparable sales approach. In contested matters in which the comparable sales approach is used, the parties often dispute the appropriate methodology, income assumptions, and the rate to be applied in converting anticipated income to present value.

3.2.3 Cost Approach

Among the recognized real estate valuation approaches, the cost approach is the least commonly used. As the North Carolina Supreme Court summarized, "[T]he cost approach involves a determination of the fair market value of the (vacant) land, the cost of reproduction of the buildings or replacement thereof by new buildings of modern design and materials less depreciation."[15] The cost approach generally is not used when sufficient data are available for developing a valuation using the comparable sales or income approach, as

---

12. *Id.* at 394, 109 S.E.2d at 231–32.

13. AMERICAN INSTITUTE OF REAL ESTATE APPRAISERS, THE APPRAISAL OF REAL ESTATE 419–21 (10th ed. 1992); *see* Dep't of Transp. v. Fleming, 112 N.C. App. 580, 583, 436 S.E.2d 407, 409 (1993) ("Under the income approach, an appraiser calculates the economic rent the property earns and deducts normal operating expenses to arrive at net income. That figure is then capitalized by a rate of return to determine the fair market value of the property").

14. *See, e.g.,* City of Charlotte v. Hurlahe, 178 N.C. App. 144, 149–51, 631 S.E.2d 28, 31 (2006) (valuing property useful for valet parking lot).

15. Redevelopment Comm'n of High Point v. Denny Roll & Panel Co., 273 N.C. 368, 370–71, 159 S.E.2d 861, 863 (1968).

these approaches are considered to more accurately reflect current market information. The cost approach may be the best method to use for a unique property for which there is insufficient market information about comparable properties.[16]

3.3 Date as to Which Value Is Measured

As explained throughout this chapter, compensation for property acquired through exercise of eminent domain is based on changes in a property's market value determined according to recognized real estate valuation methods. Property values and real estate markets change and fluctuate, and the date as to which value is determined is an important part of the valuation. G.S. 40A-63 specifies that "[t]he determination of the amount of compensation shall reflect the value of the property immediately prior to the filing of . . . the complaint under G.S. 40A-41 and except as provided in the following sections shall not reflect an increase or decrease due to the condemnation. The day of the filing of a . . . complaint shall be the date of valuation of the interest taken." This is consistent with common law. The North Carolina courts have held that the date of valuation is when the complaint is filed, except when the taking is deemed to have occurred earlier because the government took possession of or appropriated the property before filing the complaint.[17] As noted in section 3.14 below, the valuation date may not necessarily be the same as the date from which interest is calculated.

---

16. American Institute of Real Estate Appraisers, The Appraisal of Real Estate 316 (10th ed. 1992).

17. Greensboro–High Point Airport Auth. v. Irvin, 306 N.C. 263, 270, 293 S.E.2d 149, 154 (1982).

3.4 Valuation of Partial Takings

When a part of a tract is acquired for a public project, the value of the remainder of the tract could be diminished or enhanced by the project for which the property is being taken. For example, large towers and high voltage wires on a residential parcel could have a negative impact on the parcel's value.[18] Similarly, changes in drainage as a result of road widening could have a negative economic impact on property over which the drainage flows.[19] On the other hand, the extension of public utilities or highways could enhance the value of the parcels from which a portion was taken for the improvements. The Chapter 40A statute that applies when local government acquires part of a tract addresses these possibilities by providing that compensation is the greater of two measures.[20] The first measure is "the amount by which the fair market value of the entire tract immediately before the taking exceeds the fair market value of the remainder immediately after the taking."[21] As described in section 3.5.2 below, the remainder's value for compensation purposes includes the effect of economic benefits caused by the proposed project. The second measure is "the fair market value of the property taken."[22] Consequently, if the rights taken do not appreciably diminish the remainder's value or the proposed project enhances rather than diminishes the remainder's value, the owner can recover an amount equal to the value of the property taken. With this measure the possible benefits of the proposed project are not a factor in valuing the property taken.

3.5 Effect of Public Improvements

As described throughout this book, the United States Constitution requires that "just compensation" be paid to owners from whom property is taken, and the North Carolina courts have interpreted the North Carolina Constitution as having the same requirement. As discussed throughout this chapter, just

---

18. Nantahala Power & Light Co. v. Carringer, 220 N.C. 57, 59–60, 16 S.E.2d 453, 454–55 (1941).

19. Dep't of Transp. v. Bragg, 308 N.C. 367, 369–70, 302 S.E.2d 227, 229–30 (1983).

20. N.C GEN. STAT. ANN. § 40A-64(b) (2007) (hereinafter G.S.).

21. G.S. 40A-64(b)(i).

22. G.S. 40A-64(b)(ii).

compensation is based on the fair market value of the property or property rights taken, or when only part of a tract is taken, the difference in fair market value of the property before and after the taking. These value determinations are measured as of the date the complaint is filed. When an eminent domain proceeding is commenced, knowledge about the public improvement for which the government is acquiring the property could affect the property's value. The extent to which public improvements are considered in determining just compensation depends on both constitutional requirements and statutory authorization.

3.5.1 Property Taken

The public improvement for which the property is acquired is not considered in the valuation of the tract when it is taken in its entirety or in the valuation of the entire tract before a portion of it is taken.[23] For example, if property is taken for a road, the property taken—whether it is an entire parcel or only part of it—would be valued in its condition before road construction. G.S. 40A-65 specifies three circumstances that are not to be considered when valuing the property taken or when valuing the entire tract before a portion of it is taken. First, the valuation should not be affected by "the proposed improvement or project for which the property is taken."[24] Second, the valuation should not be affected by "the reasonable likelihood that the property would be acquired for that improvement or project."[25] Third, the valuation should not be affected by "the condemnation proceeding in which the property is taken."[26] The North Carolina Court of Appeals has described these rules as "intended to level the playing field and ensure that neither party receives a windfall as a result of the condemnation."[27]

G.S. 40A-65(b) also has a rule that applies if a condemnor takes property in addition to what was initially taken as a result of an expansion of or change in the project. If additional property is taken before project completion, the value of the additional property is not diminished by any of the three circumstances described in the preceding paragraph, but the valuation does take into

---

23. Piedmont Triad Regional Water Auth. v. Unger, 154 N.C. App. 589, 592–93, 572 S.E.2d 832, 835 (2002).
24. G.S. 40A-65(a)(i).
25. G.S. 40A-65(a)(ii).
26. G.S. 40A-65(a)(iii).
27. *Unger*, 154 N.C. App. at 593, 572 S.E.2d at 835 .

account "an increase in value before the date on which it became reasonably likely that the expansion or change of the project would occur, if the increase is caused by" any of these circumstances.[28]

The statute also provides that "a decrease in value before the date of valuation which is caused by physical deterioration of the property within the reasonable control of the property owner, and by his unjustified neglect, may be considered in determining value."[29]

In *Piedmont Triad Regional Water Authority v. Unger*,[30] the North Carolina Court of Appeals interpreted G.S. 40A-65 expansively to include a particular land use regulation as one of the circumstances not to be considered in the valuation if the regulation is deemed to have been adopted as part of the project. The court held that a watershed ordinance restricting development on an owner's property was related to a dam construction project for which part of the owner's property was later acquired, and the owner could therefore introduce evidence of the property's value as unaffected by the previously adopted restrictions.[31]

3.5.2 Remaining Property

Public improvements can enhance the value of property still owned after a partial acquisition. The North Carolina Supreme Court has held that considering such benefits in the compensation valuation does not violate the constitutional requirement of just compensation. As the court said, "Compensation is had when the balance is struck between the damages and benefits conferred on him by the act complained of. To that, and that alone, he has a constitutional and vested right."[32] Therefore, the General Assembly has discretion to define the extent to which an owner's award is diminished by enhanced value accruing as a result of the project for which property is taken.[33]

The cases have described two kinds of benefits resulting from eminent domain: "general benefits" and "special benefits." General benefits "'arise from the fulfillment of the public object which justified the taking [and] . . . which result[] from the enjoyment of the facilities provided by the new

---

28. G.S. 40A-65(b).
29. G.S. 40A-65(c).
30. 154 N.C. App. 589, 572 S.E.2d 832 (2002).
31. *Id.* at 591–97, 572 S.E.2d at 834–37.
32. Miller v. City of Asheville, 112 N.C. 759, 768, 16 S.E. 762, 764 (1893).
33. *Id.*

public work and from the increased general prosperity resulting from such enjoyment.'"[34] "Examples include the rise in property value due to increased traffic flow, an aesthetic upgrading of a neighborhood, or more convenient parking."[35] Consideration of general benefits to the owner has been held not to violate principles of just compensation. As the North Carolina Supreme Court explained, "Allowing the fact-finder to consider 'general benefits' follows not only persuasive authority and long practice, it also fulfils the purpose underlying the requirement of just compensation: to ensure that persons being required to provide land for public projects are put in the same financial position as prior to the taking."[36]

Special benefits "arise from the peculiar relation of the land in question to the public improvement."[37] "An example is the rise in property value due to newly acquired frontage on a public street."[38] The courts have held that special benefits also are appropriately considered in the valuation of an owner's remaining property. As the North Carolina Supreme Court noted, "It would therefore seem to be clear from the authorities that in a condemnation proceeding special benefits are to be considered as an offset, deduction or counterclaim against damages accruing to the property owner in order to determine what sum, if any, the property owner shall receive for the land so taken."[39] However, an owner cannot be required to pay if the benefits exceed what is taken. As the court said, "[T]he law does not contemplate that a city can take the property of a landowner for public purposes, pay nothing for the land taken, and at the same time recover a judgment against the owner for the privilege of having his land taken without compensation. In other words, special benefits are allowed by the law as an offset or deduction from the amount of damages to be paid, for taking the property, and to the extent only

---

34. Kirkman v. State Highway Comm'n, 257 N.C. 428, 434, 126 S.E.2d 107, 112 (1962) (quoting Templeton v. State Highway Comm'n, 254 N.C. 337, 341, 118 S.E.2d 918, 922 (1961)).

35. Dep't of Transp. v. Rowe, 353 N.C. 671, 677, 549 S.E.2d 203, 208 (2001).

36. *Id.* When the state takes part of a property, both general and special benefits are considered in the valuation. *Id.*; G.S. 136-112.

37. *Kirkman*, 257 N.C. at 433, 126 S.E.2d at 112 (quoting *Templeton*, 254 N.C. at 341, 118 S.E.2d at 922).

38. *Rowe*, 353 N.C. at 677, 549 S.E.2d at 208.

39. Goode v. City of Asheville, 193 N.C. 134, 137, 136 S.E. 340, 342 (1927); *see also* Stamey v. Town of Burnsville, 189 N.C. 39, 41, 126 S.E. 103, 104 (1925) (just coompensation "is such compensation after special benefits peculiar to the land are set off against damages").

of determining the amount the landowner shall receive for his property."[40] The North Carolina Supreme Court synthesized the analysis in *Barnes v. North Carolina State Highway Commission*,[41] when it said that "[w]here a portion of a tract of land is taken for highway purposes, the just compensation to which the landowner is entitled is the difference between the fair market value of the property *as a whole* immediately before and immediately after the appropriation of the portion thereof. In arriving at this difference consideration must be given to the general and special benefits accruing to the landowner with respect to the land not taken. That difference includes everything which affects the value of the property taken in relation to the *entire* property affected."[42]

The benefits analysis does not attempt to account for the effects of *all* public improvements having a possible economic connection to the subject property. As the North Carolina Supreme Court explained, "Whether benefits are general or special, 'it is generally agreed that only those benefits can be taken into consideration which arise from the particular improvement for the purpose of which the owner's land is taken or damaged and not those which have no causal connection with such improvements but are derived from other previous or subsequent improvements, even though made by the condemnor.'"[43]

Consistent with the case law, the compensation required under Chapter 40A as a result of a local government condemnation of part of a tract takes into account both general and special benefits to the remaining tract. G.S. 40A-66(a) provides as follows: "If there is a taking of less than the entire tract, the value of the remainder on the valuation date shall reflect increases or decreases in value caused by the proposed project including any work to be performed under an agreement between the parties." A further qualification is set forth in G.S. 40A-66(b), which provides that "[t]he value of the remainder, as of the date of valuation, shall reflect the time the damage or benefit caused by the proposed improvement or project will be actually realized."

The condemnor has the burden of proving any offsetting benefits.[44]

---

40. *Goode*, 193 N.C. at 137, 136 S.E. at 342.

41. 250 N.C. 378, 109 S.E.2d 219 (1959).

42. *Id.* at 383, 109 S.E.2d at 224 (emphasis in original).

43. Kirkman v. State Highway Comm'n, 257 N.C. 428, 433, 126 S.E.2d 107, 111 (1962) (quoting ANNO., EMINENT DOMAIN—DEDUCTION OF BENEFITS, 145 A.L.R. 110).

44. *Kirkman*, 257 N.C. at 434, 126 S.E.2d at 112.

3.6 Affected Property

Owners and condemnors often dispute what constitutes the boundaries of the property considered affected by a taking. The statutes governing local government condemnation, Chapter 40A, employ the concept of "an integrated economic unit" to define what constitutes the property affected for the purpose of determining just compensation. G.S. 40A-67 provides as follows: "For the purpose of determining compensation under this Article, all contiguous tracts of land that are in the same ownership and are being used as an integrated economic unit shall be treated as if the combined tracts constitute a single tract." Application of this direction requires consideration of the case law regarding what constitutes "same ownership," "contiguous," and "an integrated economic unit." These are legal rather than factual questions. As the North Carolina Supreme Court noted, "Ordinarily the question, whether two or more parcels of land constitute one tract for the purpose of assessing damages for injury to the portion not taken or offsetting benefits against damages, is one of law for the court. "[45] The North Carolina courts have looked at ownership of the subject parcels, their physical relationship, and the manner in which they are used. The most comprehensive discussion of this analysis under North Carolina law was provided in *Barnes v. North Carolina State Highway Commission*.[46] The court said that "[t]he factors most generally emphasized are unity of ownership, physical unity and unity of use. Under certain circumstances the presence of all these unities is not essential. The respective importance of these factors depends upon the factual situation in individual cases."[47] This approach is sometimes referred to as The Rule of the Three Unities.

3.6.1 Ownership Unity

Questions about ownership unity arise when some but not all of the same ownership interests hold adjoining parcels. For example, a corporation that owned a vacant industrial lot was held incapable of unified ownership with a partnership owning adjacent lots, despite the fact that a partner also was a principal shareholder of the corporation.[48] However, when closely

---

45. *Barnes*, 250 N.C. at 384, 109 S.E.2d at 224.
46. 250 N.C. 378, 109 S.E.2d 219 (1959).
47. *Id*. at 384, 109 S.E.2d at 224–25.
48. Dep't of Transp. v. Roymac Partnership, 158 N.C. App. 403, 581 S.E.2d 770 (2003).

interlocking partnerships owned lots intended for development as an "integrated economic unit," the North Carolina Court of Appeals held that minor variations in the identity of the partnerships did not destroy ownership unity for purposes of assessing just compensation.[49] In an expansive view of unity, in *City of Winston-Salem v. Yarbrough*[50] the court of appeals held that spouses' separately owned properties were in unified ownership based on their reciprocal inchoate marital property interests and a common development plan.[51] In *City of Winston-Salem v. Slate*,[52] the court of appeals held that ownership unity could be satisfied when the co-owners of one lot were among the co-owners of an adjacent tract, quoting the following from *Barnes*: "'It is not a requisite for unity of ownership that a party have the same quantity or quality of interest or estate in all parts of the tract. But where there are tenants in common, one or more of the tenants must own some interest and estate in the entire tract'."[53]

3.6.2 Physical Unity

Ordinarily parcels that are physically separate cannot be considered a single unit. If property has been subdivided and only a part of it is acquired in the condemnation, the owner will not be entitled to compensation for any alleged diminution in value to the other parts of what was previously a unified parcel. But as the North Carolina Supreme Court explained, "[I]n exceptional cases, where there is an indivisible unity of use, owners have been permitted to include parcels in condemnation proceedings that are physically separate and to treat them as a unit."[54] The court also noted that "[i]t is generally held that parcels of land separated by an established city street, in use by the public, are separate and independent as a matter of law."[55]

---

49. Dep't of Transp. v. Nelson Co., 127 N.C. App. 365, 367, 489 S.E.2d 449, 450 (1997).

50. 117 N.C. App. 340, 451 S.E.2d 358 (1994).

51. *Id.* at 344–45, 451 S.E.2d at 362–63.

52. ___N.C. App.___, 647 S.E.2d 643 (2007).

53. *Id.* at ___, 647 S.E.2d at 650 (quoting *Barnes*, 250 N.C. at 384, 109 S.E.2d at 225 (emphasis omitted)).

54. Barnes v. North Carolina State Highway Comm'n, 250 N.C. 378, 385, 109 S.E.2d 219, 225 (1959).

55. *Id.*

3.6.3 Use Unity

The North Carolina Supreme Court has said that "[u]sually unity of use is given greatest emphasis."[56] As the court explained, "If the uses of two or more sections of land are different and inconsistent, no claim of unity can be maintained. But the mere possibility of adaptability to different uses will not render segments of land separate and independent."[57] Parcels owned for phased development of an integrated complex may be sufficiently unified in intended use,[58] but not when subsequent phases are planned only after completed development of the land from which rights were acquired by eminent domain.[59] The court also has noted that "[m]ere paper division, lot or property lines, and undeveloped streets and alleys are not sufficient alone to destroy the unity of land."[60]

3.7 Several Interests and Extraction Rights

When government acquires an entire tract by eminent domain, the property is valued as a whole without regard to separate ownership interests in the tract. As the North Carolina Supreme Court noted,

> "The rule is generally recognized (though not invariably followed) that, where there are several interests or estates in a parcel of real estate taken by eminent domain, a proper method of fixing the value of, or damage to, each interest or estate, is to determine the value of, or damage to, the property as a whole, and then to apportion the same among the several owners according to their respective interests or estates, rather than to take each interest or estate as a unit and fix the value thereof, or damage thereto, separately."[61]

Therefore, although a condemnor must include the owners of several interests as defendants in the eminent domain proceeding, the compensation will be based on the parcel's value as if it had a single owner.

---

56. *Id.* at 384, 109 S.E.2d at 224–25.

57. *Id.* at 385, 109 S.E.2d at 225.

58. Dep't of Transp. v. Nelson Co., 127 N.C. App. 365, 368–69, 489 S.E.2d 449, 450–51 (1997).

59. Bd. of Transp. v. Martin, 296 N.C. 20, 30, 249 S.E.2d 390, 397 (1978).

60. Barnes v. North Carolina State Highway Comm'n, 250 N.C. 378, 385, 109 S.E.2d 219, 225 (1959).

61. Barnes v. North Carolina State Highway Comm'n, 257 N.C. 507, 520, 126 S.E.2d 732, 741–42 (1962) (quoting 18 Am. Jur. *Eminent Domain* § 239).

When land has valuable minerals or other materials that could be extracted, the owner is entitled to payment of market value for the parcel as a whole, not the aggregate of the land and materials sold separately. However, in *City of Hillsborough v. Hughes*,[62] the court of appeals rejected an argument that this means an expert cannot assign a value to minerals within the context of valuing the parcel as a whole. The court said, "Preventing an appraiser witness from disclosing such information seems to be at odds with the practice of real estate appraisal, and prevents an accurate reflection for the jury of the fair market value of the condemned property."[63] The court of appeals "concluded that it is proper to consider separate values in determining the fair market value of the property as a whole. As indicated in the instruction, once that fair market value is determined, the jury may not then add any amount for separate enhancing components of the property, which then, would constitute double counting."[64] These distinctions about the proper consideration of separate valuation components can be confusing. When compensation is being decided by a jury, the jury instructions must be prepared carefully to avoid potential misapplication of separate valuation component testimony.

If only the minerals are being taken by eminent domain, as the North Carolina Court of Appeals explained, "The general rule in valuing the minerals on a tract of land being taken for public use is that the presence of mineable minerals on the land should be taken into consideration when appraising the fair market value of the land, but the minerals should not be valued separately then added onto the fair market value of the land as currently used. An exception to this rule is recognized where the minerals alone are taken or the rights to the minerals are held by someone other than the holder of the fee."[65] The value of the minerals separately owned is their unexcavated value, which means taking into account the costs of extraction and removal from the premises.[66] The court of appeals said that "[f]actors bearing on this determination would be (i) potential tonnage, (ii) cost of extracting the sand and gravel, (iii) amount of royalty to be paid under the agreement, (iv) cost of transporting and processing the sand and gravel and (v) an available market value for sale of the sand and gravel."[67]

---

62. 140 N.C. App. 714, 538 S.E.2d 586 (2000).

63. *Id.* at 718, 538 S.E.2d at 588.

64. *Id.* at 720, 538 S.E.2d at 589.

65. *In re* Lee, 85 N.C. App. 302, 305, 354 S.E.2d 759, 762 (1987) (citation omitted).

66. *Id.* at 306, 354 S.E.2d at 762.

67. *Id.*

Improvements, timber, or fixtures removed and retained by an owner would not be included in the value of the property taken. G.S. 40A-64(c) provides: "If the owner is to be allowed to remove any timber, building or other permanent improvement, or fixtures from the property, the value thereof shall not be included in the compensation award, but the cost of removal shall be considered as an element to be compensated."

3.8   Loss of Business Income

When land on which a business is operated is taken and the business operations must be moved or curtailed, owners may believe they have lost a promising profit stream from the business at its existing location. Although future profit is always subject to various contingencies and in many cases a business could be operated at least as profitably at a new location, those whose businesses are affected by condemnation sometimes argue that they should be compensated for their estimate of lost anticipated income based on forecasts derived from presently known financial information. For some damage claims, such as negligence and breach of a contract, the law allows recovery of lost business income if it can be calculated with reasonable certainty.[68] But the statutes defining compensation for property taken through eminent domain do not include estimated lost business profits. The general rule applied by the courts, subject to limited exceptions involving unusual uses of eminent domain, "is that loss of profits from the operation of a business conducted on the property is not an element of recoverable damages in an award pursuant to an eminent domain taking."[69] The statutes governing local government eminent domain also do not include business relocation expenses as part of the required compensation, and the courts have held that such expenses are not recoverable in the absence of a statutory requirement or agreement.[70]

---

68. Tillis v. Calvine Cotton Mills Inc., 251 N.C. 359, 366, 111 S.E.2d 606, 612 (1959) ("[A]bsolute certainty is not required but evidence of damages must be sufficiently specific and complete to permit the jury to arrive at a reasonable conclusion").

69. Dep't of Transp. v. Fleming, 112 N.C. App. 580, 582, 436 S.E.2d 407, 409 (1993).

70. Williams v. State Highway Comm'n, 252 N.C. 141, 145, 113 S.E.2d 263, 267 (1960).

The distinction between diminished real estate value, for which an owner must be compensated, and lost business profits, which have been held not to be compensable, can be difficult to discern. As described in section 3.2.2 above, the income approach to valuing commercial real estate involves calculating income that the real estate is anticipated to generate using such information as market rents, vacancy rates, and maintenance and operating costs. This approach reflects market realities. A prospective purchaser will want to know the rent and other income history of commercial property to analyze reasonably anticipated profit, and this information will be the basis for calculating a reasonable price to pay for the property. Market values should reflect such realities. On the other hand, the courts have made clear that the federal and state constitutions require payment for the real estate taken and not for anticipated lost business profits.

Analytical difficulty arises when part of the owner's land is taken. The part taken could restrict the owner's business, as might occur, for instance, if the result is less rental or parking space. In *Kirkman v. State Highway Commission*,[71] the North Carolina Supreme Court held that "[l]oss of profits or injury to a growing business conducted on property or connected therewith are not elements of recoverable damages in an award for the taking under the power of eminent domain. However, when the taking renders the remaining land unfit or less valuable for any use to which it is adapted, that factor is a proper item to be considered in determining whether the taking has diminished the value of the land itself."[72] The court therefore indicated that the diminished business capacity of the site was an appropriate consideration. However, a divided supreme court later reiterated that what it considers to be "business profits" are not compensable. The case, *Department of Transportation v. M.M. Fowler Inc.*,[73] involved an owner's claim to compensation for changes to entrance points for a property used for a gas station and convenience store. The jury heard testimony from an expert who, in using an income approach to valuation, calculated value based on the owner's estimate of lost profits. The supreme court said that this "quantified lost business profits" testimony, and any valuation based solely on that evidence, should not have been permitted.[74] The court said, "Doing so suggests to the jury that the

---

71. 257 N.C. 428, 126 S.E.2d 107 (1962).
72. *Id.* at 432, 126 S.E.2d at 110 (citation omitted).
73. 361 N.C. 1, 637 S.E.2d 885 (2006).
74. *Id.* at 13–15, 637 S.E.2d at 894–95.

property owner is entitled to those losses."[75] The court noted that the income approach may be an appropriate valuation method, but "with the income approach, the appraisal must differentiate between income directly from the property and profits of the business located on the land."[76] The distinction between "income directly from the property" and "profits of the business located on the land" may be difficult to discern, but the supreme court has made clear that a distinction must be maintained.[77]

3.9 Easements

The eminent domain valuation analysis can be particularly contentious when the condemnor acquires an easement on an owner's property, as occurs with road expansions and the installation of sewer and utility lines. The economic effect of an easement on property, as calculated by an appraiser, often is not

---

75. *Id.* at 12, 637 S.E.2d at 894.

76. *Id.* at 13, 637 S.E.2d at 894. Three dissenting justices disagreed with what they described as the majority's adoption of a "per se ban" on the admission of evidence of lost revenue "when the property itself contributes in a direct way to the revenue derived from a tract adapted to its highest and best use." *Id.* at 15–26, 637 S.E.2d at 895–902 (Martin, J., dissenting). The dissent approved of the following instruction given by the trial court: "Loss of profits or injury to a growing business conducted on property or connected therewith are not elements of recoverable damages and an award for the taking under the power of eminent domain. However, when the taking renders the remaining land unfit or less valuable for any use to which it is adapted, that fact is a proper item to be consider[ed] in determining whether the taking has diminished the value of the land itself." *Id.* at 23, 637 S.E.2d at 900.

77. In *M.M. Fowler* the owner's valuation did not follow the common methodology for the income approach to real estate valuation. The owner argued that changes to the property required lowering the price of gas to attract customers. According to the owner's witness, this resulted in a loss of four cents per gallon of profit, or $90,000 per year, for a $540,000 reduction after multiplying a "conservative factor" of six. The Department of Transportation estimated the impact of the taking on the site to be $166,850. The jury awarded $450,000. 361 N.C. at 3–4, 12, 637 S.E.2d at 888, 893–94. Although the owner's approach is based on a contention about loss of the site's profitability as a gas station, the computation reflects the kind of simplified calculation sometimes used in claims to loss of income in tort and contract cases, not standard real estate market valuation methodology, which involves a number of market factors as described in section 3.2.2 above.

as great as owners perceive it to be. The amount of compensation is based on the diminished value of the property on which the easement is taken. As the North Carolina Supreme Court explained,

> The purpose of the law is to compensate the landowner for his loss resulting from the imposition of the easement. It seeks to place him in the same financial condition, as respects the particular land in question, as he was before the easement was imposed. The market value is the yardstick by which such loss is measured. The owner must be paid such an amount as will equal, when added to the reasonable market value of the land after the imposition of the easement, its reasonable market value just prior to the taking. It follows of necessity that the depreciation in value, if any, of the tract of land outside the bounds of the easement is to be considered in assessing the amount to be paid and that whether the imposition of such easement is detrimental to the remaining land is essentially a question of fact.[78]

When a temporary easement is taken, such as a temporary construction easement used to move or store equipment on someone's land, the valuation might appropriately consider the fair rental value of the easement area during the time of use; costs incurred by the owner in removing or altering improvements to accommodate the government's use; the costs to the owner of alternative access; the value of removed trees, crops, or other improvements; and any resulting diminished value to the owner's remaining property.[79]

If the condemnor's acquisition of property results in someone's loss of easement rights, the easement holder would be entitled to compensation for the diminution in value to the property benefited by the easement.[80]

---

78. Nantahala Power & Light Co. v. Carringer, 220 N.C. 57, 59, 16 S.E.2d 453, 454–55 (1941).

79. Colonial Pipeline Co. v. Weaver, 310 N.C. 93, 107, 310 S.E.2d 338, 346 (1984).

80. United States v. Welch, 217 U.S. 333 (1910).

3.10 Leases

Property taken or affected by eminent domain could have occupying tenants with rights acquired by written agreements or through informal arrangements, such as at-will or month-to-month tenancies. Commercial properties are likely to involve formal lease arrangements, and notice of long-term leases is likely to be recorded at the register of deeds. Lessees of such leases are likely to be necessary parties in an eminent domain proceeding, and they may have rights to a part of the condemnation award if their interests are affected by the taking. As the North Carolina Supreme Court noted, "When condemned land is subject to a leasehold estate the tenant is entitled to share in the award since the value of his interest is a part of the value of the fee."[81] The condemnor pays only one amount for the property taken, and the relative entitlement of the landlord and tenant to share in the compensation is a matter of allocation between them. In other words, the condemnor does not pay twice. As the North Carolina Supreme Court explained,

> [W]hen an entire piece of property is acquired by condemners, the sovereign must pay the reasonable market value for it. It is not required to pay an additional amount to a lessee, life tenant, or others having an interest, contingent, vested, or otherwise. While an advantageous lease is a proper factor to be considered—just as the fact that the property is not rented, or is unrentable, would be—in determining its fair market value, the condemner's total liability is fixed when the fair market value of the property, considering all proper factors, has been established.[82]

The tenant may have a right to compensation, but that right is against the landlord, not the condemnor. As the court further explained, "[T]he owner is required to account to his lessee for the value of his lease."[83] Many leases specifically address allocation of compensation awards between the lessor and lessee.

When property subject to leases is taken and a lease is prematurely terminated as a result of the taking, a party to the lease may believe that an

---

81. Ross v. Perry, 281 N.C. 570, 576, 189 S.E.2d 226, 229 (1972).

82. City of Durham v. Eastern Realty Co., 270 N.C. 631, 635, 155 S.E.2d 231, 234 (1967).

83. *Id.*

economic advantage has been lost. A landlord entitled to rents higher than market value may believe that premature termination has diminished a favorable income stream, and a tenant who occupied space with an agreement for rents lower than market value may believe that premature termination will be costly. The North Carolina Supreme Court has instructed that "[w]hen rental property is condemned the owner may not recover for lost rents, but rental value of property is competent upon the question of the fair market value of the property at the time of the taking."[84] An owner may therefore be able to show that the property value should take into account the higher-than-market income stream.

With respect to the tenant's possible share in the award, the court has explained that "[o]rdinarily the value of a lease is the difference between the rental value of the unexpired term and the rent reserved in the lease. If a forfeited lease is worth nothing more than the stipulated rent, the lessee has sustained no damage. He suffers a loss only when his lease is worth more than the rent he pays, that is, only when his lease is a bargain. Thus, when the owner of the fee is required to divide a compensation award with the owner of the leasehold he is not receiving rent from the lease but is, in effect, paying a penalty for it."[85]

3.11 Life Estates

If the property that the government acquires by eminent domain is subject to a life estate, the life tenant's right of occupancy is affected as well as the residual rights of those who will become owners after the life tenant's death. These different interests do not affect the condemnor's obligation to pay the fair market value of the property taken. Recognizing the loss suffered by the life tenant, courts have subjected the damage award to a trust for the tenant's benefit. The damages award effectively takes the place of the real estate; the award is held in trust with the income paid to the life tenant, and upon the life tenant's death is distributed to those with the right to the remainder.[86]

---

84. Kirkman v. State Highway Comm'n, 257 N.C. 428, 432, 126 S.E.2d 107, 110 (1962).

85. *Ross*, 281 N.C. at 576, 189 S.E.2d at 229 (citations omitted).

86. Redevelopment Comm'n of the City of Greenville v. Capehart, 268 N.C. 114, 150 S.E.2d 62 (1966).

The statutes governing local government condemnation give broad authority to the commissioners, jury, or judges to include in a judgment essential parameters for the manner in which this arrangement is to be carried out. Chapter 40A authorizes that "[t]he award be apportioned and distributed on the basis of the respective values of the interests of the life tenant and remainderman," "[t]he compensation be used to purchase comparable property to be held subject to the life tenancy," "[t]he compensation be held in trust and administered subject to the terms of the instrument that created the life tenancy," or "[a]ny other equitable arrangement be carried out."[87]

3.12 Real Estate Liens

Loan agreements between real estate owners and lenders often will specify how eminent domain proceedings affect the status of the security instrument and the parties' relative rights to condemnation awards. Deeds of trust and other security instruments typically provide that the lender is entitled to receive condemnation proceeds and apply them to the secured debt. If an entire parcel is taken, the secured lender will want to apply the proceeds to payment of the secured debt. Secured lenders often assert a right to the proceeds even if only part of the secured premises is taken or if limited rights, such as easements, are acquired by eminent domain. In any event secured lenders will seek assurance that after the taking the extent of their security, in relation to the outstanding amount of the secured debt, is not impaired.

The North Carolina statutes governing the exercise of eminent domain by local government contain two provisions specifically affecting the relationship between a secured creditor and landowner which expressly override any agreement between the two. The first provides that in the case of a partial taking, "the lienholder may share in the amount of compensation awarded only to the extent determined by the commissioners or by the jury or by the judge to be necessary to prevent an impairment of his security, and the lien shall continue upon the part of the property not taken as security for the unpaid portion of the indebtedness until it is paid."[88] By operation of this provision, the finder of fact would at the appropriate time consider the question of whether the lender's security interest has been impaired by the taking and the value of any such impairment, which would represent the secured lender's share of the

---

87. G.S. 40A-69.
88. G.S. 40A-68(1).

condemnation proceeds. The second provision invalidates prepayment penalties on account of an eminent domain proceeding, stating that "[n]either the condemnor nor owner is liable to the lienholder for any penalty for prepayment of the debt secured by the lien, and the amount awarded by the judgment to the lienholder shall not include any penalty therefor."[89]

3.13 Relocation Assistance

Owners forced to move their residences or relocate as a result of a government project sometimes believe that the payment for their real estate is inadequate if it does not take into account moving expenses and costs of relocation. The courts generally have held that reimbursement of such expenses is not constitutionally required.[90] Since 1970 the federal Uniform Relocation Assistance and Real Property Acquisition Policies Act[91] has required federal agencies to reimburse owners for many such expenses, and federal law requires states to do so when the taking is in connection with a federal project or a project receiving federal financial assistance. The applicable requirements are set forth in Chapter 61 of Title 42, United States Code,[92] and rules and schedules under Title 49, Part 24, Code of Federal Regulations. The United States Department of Transportation is the lead agency for administering these laws, and the department has delegated its responsibility to the Federal Highway Administration. Within the administration relocation assistance is handled by the Office of Real Estate Services.[93]

North Carolina has a similar statute that applies to state eminent domain actions: the Uniform Relocation Assistance and Real Property Acquisition Policies Act, Article 2 of Chapter 133.[94] The act's stated purpose is "to establish a uniform policy for the fair and equitable treatment of persons displaced as a result of public works programs in order that such persons shall not suffer disproportionate injuries as a result of programs designed for the benefit of

---

89. G.S. 40A-68(2).

90. Williams v. State Highway Comm'n, 252 N.C. 141, 145, 113 S.E.2d 263, 267 (1960).

91. 42 U.S.C. §§ 4601–4655 (2000).

92. *Id.*

93. Links to rules and schedules can be found at www.fhwa.dot.gov/realestate/ua/index.htm (last visited March 27, 2008).

94. G.S. 133-5 through G.S. 133-18.

the public as a whole and to insure continuing eligibility for federal aid funds to the State and its agencies and subdivisions."[95] The state law applies to local government governing bodies, agencies, commissions, and authorities.[96] The rules promulgated by the North Carolina Department of Transportation incorporate the federal rules.[97] Local governments are not required to provide the Uniform Act's defined payments for moving and related expenses or replacement housing "unless federal law makes such payments a condition of federal funding."[98] Local governments must therefore comply if they are part of a project undertaken by a federal agency or with federal financial assistance.

Amounts paid according to the Uniform Act are considered "administrative payments." The statute expressly disclaims any intent to treat such payments as constitutionally required just compensation.[99] Furthermore, it states that nothing contained in the Uniform Act "shall be construed as creating any right enforceable in any court and the determination of the agency under the procedure provided" in the statute "shall be conclusive and not subject to judicial review."[100]

The Uniform Act directs condemnors to plan projects in a way that minimizes the adverse impact of displacing individuals, families, businesses, and farm operations and to provide advisory services to those who are displaced.[101] The statutes generally allow payment either of actual reasonable expenses for moving and relocation or a lump sum according to a schedule determined by the acquiring agency. For example, both federal and state law provide for payment of "[a]ctual reasonable expenses necessary to reestablish a displaced farm, nonprofit organization, or small business at its new site . . . but not to exceed

95. G.S. 133-6.

96. G.S. 133-7(1).

97. By rule the North Carolina Department of Transportation incorporates "49 CFR Subpart 24 and 23 CFR Subpart C, including subsequent amendments and editions." 19A N.C.A.C. 02B.0432. At this date the federal rules for relocation assistance are in 49 C.F.R. Part 24, Subparts C–F. 23 C.F.R. Chapter 1, Subchapter C, provides rules regarding compliance with the federal civil rights laws in federal and federally assisted projects. The federal rules define the nature of expenses for which reimbursement will be made and generally provide for an alternative lump sum payment according to a schedule.

98. G.S. 133-18.

99. G.S. 133-17.

100. *Id.*

101. *Id.*

ten thousand dollars ($10,000)"[102] or a lump sum payment of between $1,000 and $20,000 according to criteria established by the agency.[103] Homeowners may be allowed an additional payment of up to $22,500 for replacement housing actually acquired, which is intended to address the costs of comparable housing or provide compensation for increased mortgage expenses for the homeowner to obtain a new loan for the replacement dwelling.[104] Tenants also may be allowed an additional sum of up to $5,250 for costs in connection with replacement housing.[105]

A significant number of local government units have voluntarily adopted relocation assistance programs, modeled after the state and federal laws, to provide benefits to residents and business owners displaced as a result of property acquisitions.

3.14 Interest

Under Chapter 40A, the condemnor is required to deposit the amount of estimated just compensation when the complaint is filed.[106] The statute requires the court to add six percent interest to the amount awarded as compensation from the date of taking to the date of judgment, but no such interest is paid on the amount deposited into the court, which the owner may withdraw without waiving the right to challenge the amount as insufficient.[107]

The interest calculation will be based on what is considered to be the date of the taking, which generally is when the complaint is filed. For interest calculation purposes, the date of the taking is the earlier of when title vests or the date the condemnor acquires a right of possession.[108] Title vests upon the filing of the complaint when the taking is a "quick take" for the purposes specified in G.S. 40A-42. Otherwise, the date of taking is when the condemnor has a right to possession, which is consistent with how the courts awarded

---

102. 42 U.S.C. § 4622(a); G.S. 133-8(4).

103. 42 U.S.C. § 4622(c), G.S. 133-8(c).

104. 42 U.S.C. § 4623; G.S. 133-9.

105. 42 U.S.C. § 4624; G.S. 133-10.

106. G.S. 40A-53.

107. See section 2.8.9 above.

108. Dare County Bd. of Educ. v. Sakaria, 127 N.C. App 585, 587–91, 492 S.E.2d 369, 371–73 (1997).

interest prior to the statute's enactment.[109] If the owner does not answer the complaint, the condemnor acquires a right of possession 120 days after the complaint was served.[110] The condemnor also acquires a right of possession when the owner files an answer that only contests the compensation amount or withdraws the estimated compensation deposit.[111]

Payment of interest may be constitutionally required as part of just compensation. The North Carolina Supreme Court noted, "'[I]f the taking precedes the payment of compensation, the owner is entitled to such addition to the value at the time of the taking as will produce the full equivalent of such value paid contemporaneously. Interest at a proper rate is a good measure of the amount to be added.'"[112] Accordingly, if an owner establishes that property was taken by inverse condemnation before or without an eminent domain proceeding, the owner may be entitled to interest measured from the date of actual occupation.

When a rate is set by statute, as is the case for local government condemnations under Chapter 40A,[113] it is presumed to be the required reasonable compensation, but an owner may rebut this presumption and recover the rate established to be a prevailing rate for prudent investments.[114] The North Carolina Supreme Court has said that the same prudent investor analysis is appropriate for deciding whether the interest is to be simple or compound.[115]

---

109. *Id.* at 590–91, 492 S.E.2d at 373.

110. G.S. 40A-42(b); G.S. 40A-46.

111. G.S. 40A-42(b).

112. DeBruhl v. State Highway & Public Works Comm'n, 247 N.C. 671, 677–78, 102 S.E.2d 229, 234 (1958) (quoting Brooks–Scanlon Corp. v. United States, 265 U.S. 106, 123 (1924)).

113. G.S. 40A-53 (6 percent per annum).

114. Lea Co. v. North Carolina Bd. of Transp., 317 N.C. 254, 260–63, 345 S.E.2d 355, 358–60 (1986).

115. *Id.* at 264, 345 S.E.2d at 360–61.

4   Inverse Condemnation

4.1   **Origins and Nature of Inverse Condemnation   125**

4.2   **Statutory Remedy for Local Government Inverse
       Condemnation   127**

    4.2.1   Exclusivity   128

    4.2.2   Time Limit   130

    4.2.3   Unforeseeable Conditions   132

4.3   **Inverse Condemnation for Physical Intrusions   134**

4.4   **Inverse Condemnation for Changes Affecting Access   141**

4.5   **Regulatory Takings   144**

    4.5.1   Regulatory Takings Based on the United States Constitution   145

    4.5.2   North Carolina Law on Regulatory Takings   147

    4.5.3   Exactions   150

4.1 Origins and Nature of Inverse Condemnation

The government must compensate owners for property it takes. Government's occupation or use of property without having followed the eminent domain procedure is referred to as "inverse condemnation," a term that reflects the reversal of the parties' usual roles in the exchange of property rights for compensation. The landowner files an action against the government to compel it to pay for what it already took but should have first acquired by following an authorized eminent domain proceeding.

Although claims against the government for taking property without paying for it are among the earliest reported cases in North Carolina, the term "inverse condemnation" was coined only recently, in 1964. In *City of Charlotte v. Spratt*,[1] the North Carolina Supreme Court considered a landowner's claim for compensation as a result of noise from flights on approach to the Charlotte airport. The court defined *inverse condemnation* as "a term often used to designate 'a cause of action against a governmental defendant to recover the value of property which has been taken in fact by the governmental defendant, even though no formal exercise of the power of eminent domain has been attempted by the taking agency.'"[2]

Claims for compensation have arisen whenever the government has undertaken, or authorized enterprises to undertake, activities that neighboring owners believe harm their property. First mills, then railroads, and later sewage plants, highways, and airports all have been the subject of claims for compensation by neighboring property owners. The courts have tried to make meaningful distinctions between the generalized effect that neighborhoods experience as a result of public projects, for which no compensation is paid, and a more specific impact for which an owner must be compensated. As explained below, various legal theories have been employed in inverse condemnation cases, but the essence of the courts' analysis boils down to an imprecise sense of basic fairness, which has evolved as government activities have expanded and reasonable expectations about property rights have changed.

The North Carolina General Assembly early on acknowledged that landowners may be entitled to compensation when activity undertaken by

---

1. 263 N.C. 656, 140 S.E.2d 341 (1965).

2. *Id.* at 662–63, 140 S.E.2d at 346 (quoting City of Jacksonville v. Schumann, 167 So. 2d 95, 98 (Fla. App. 1964)).

government or its instrumentalities physically encroaches on an owner's property but the procedure for acquiring the rights and paying just compensation has not been followed. In the early statehood years, water mills were important to the public for grinding grains and seeds and later as a source of power. Mills divert water from its natural course, a process that can affect others who use the same water source for their mills or for irrigation. Mills also can cause erosion or pooling. To support the public interest in mill construction and operation, the General Assembly enabled operators to acquire rights at the expense of other owners. The General Assembly also authorized those adversely affected to bring an action to recover compensation if the damage was above a minimum amount.[3] When a remedy was provided by statute, the owner generally was restricted to the compensation the statute authorized. For example, the North Carolina Supreme Court upheld a statutory minimum for claims in connection with mills and rejected claims for additional compensation based on common law causes of action such as trespass.[4]

In the nineteenth century, railroads became the most common source of conflict between landowners and those empowered to build improvements deemed to benefit the general public. The North Carolina Supreme Court took the same approach it took with mills, restricting landowners to statutorily authorized compensation. For example, the court rejected efforts to stop railroad construction as a trespass, restricting owners to compensation authorized by legislation.[5]

The early mill and railroad cases typically arose in situations in which a procedure was legislatively authorized for owners to use to obtain compensation. The courts redirected owners who brought common law claims to the legislatively authorized remedies. The courts have had more trouble developing a conceptual framework for deciding when a claim can be brought in the absence of a statutory remedy. In the mill and railroad cases mentioned above, the North Carolina Supreme Court has generally held that when the General Assembly does provide a remedy for land taken in connection with a particular kind of public improvement, there are no common law remedies, including for trespass or nuisance. However, the courts in North Carolina, as in other states, commonly employed these other conceptual grounds when

---

3. Laws of 1809, ch. 15, *in* Laws of N.C., ch. 773 (1821).
4. Mumford v. Terry, 4 N.C. 308 (1816).
5. McIntyre v. Western N.C. R.R., 67 N.C. 278, 279 (1872).

analyzing a compensation claim for which no statutory remedy was available and when considering whether a government activity was sufficiently intrusive to constitute a taking. Consequently, the courts' attempts to formulate rules for property owner claims against the government have involved a confusing combination of common law and constitutional law concepts. New components are still being added to the formulation. For instance, federal law, 42 U.S.C. § 1983, now provides another possible basis for awarding compensation for a deprivation of property rights.[6] As one commentator put it, the case law addressing government liability for property damage is a "shifting, puzzling pattern," in which courts "have interwoven the law of inverse condemnation with property and tort law concepts and with artificial interpretations of eminent domain provisions."[7] As this commentator also said, "What gives inverse condemnation law its special quality is its frequent distortion of property and tort law concepts and its equally artificial interpretations of the eminent domain clause to find liability."[8] In sum, the law of inverse condemnation is an untidy compilation of legal theories.

4.2 Statutory Remedy for Local Government Inverse Condemnation

Chapter 40A prescribes a procedure for a property owner to commence a proceeding in superior court for compensation for an alleged taking by "an act or omission of a condemnor listed in G.S. 40A-3(b) or (c)."[9] As described in section 1.7, G.S. 40A-3(b) condemnors are municipalities and counties and their boards of education. As described in section 1.8, G.S. 40A-3(c) condemnors are composed of a variety of districts, boards, and other authorities organized by or among local governments. Accordingly, if these local governments or local government entities take property without bringing an eminent

---

6. *See, e.g.,* National Adver. Co. v. City of Raleigh, 947 F.2d 1158 (4th Cir. 1991), *cert. denied,* 504 U.S. 931 (1992) (Section 1983 claim for alleged taking by sign ordinance); Capital Outdoor Adver. Inc. v. City of Raleigh, 337 N.C. 150, 446 S.E.2d 289 (1994) (same).

7. Daniel R. Mandelker, *Inverse Condemnation: The Constitutional Limits of Public Responsibility,* Wisc. L. Rev. 3, 3, 16 (1966).

8. *Id.* at 8.

9. N.C. Gen. Stat. Ann. § 40A-51 (2007) (hereinafter G.S.).

domain proceeding, the owner's remedy is an action under Chapter 40A. The procedural requirements for filing such a claim are set forth in G.S. 40A-51 and are described in section 2.13. Considerations regarding the exclusivity of the Chapter 40A procedure are discussed in subsection 4.2.1 below. Time limit considerations are discussed in subsections 4.2.2 and 4.2.3 below.

4.2.1 Exclusivity

Availability of a statutory procedure usually means that the owner may not elect to pursue a common law remedy based on theories such as trespass or nuisance. This principle was first established in the early cases involving mills. For example, in *Gillet v. Jones*,[10] the landowner alleged an overflowing mill and dam created a nuisance. The North Carolina Supreme Court said that "[t]he policy of the [eminent domain] act requires its application to all injuries, of whatever character, arising from the erection of a mill, for the statute may otherwise be rendered, in a great degree, nugatory."[11] In *McIntire v. Western North Carolina Railroad*,[12] the court applied the same analysis to a trespass claim in connection with a railroad company that entered the owner's land during line construction, when by legislative act an eminent domain procedure was available. The court said, "There can be no doubt that the Legislature had the right to take away the common law remedy; the only question possible, is, as to their intention."[13] As described throughout this chapter, the courts have mixed common law theories with notions of constitutional entitlement to authorize compensation for inverse condemnation when no statutory procedure was available to the owner.[14] As described in section 4.3 below, the courts also have employed common law theories in attempting to distinguish between government activities that constitute a taking and those that do not. Since Chapter 40A was enacted in 1981, however, owners claiming entitlement to compensation for

---

10. 18 N.C. 339 (1835).

11. *Id.* at 343.

12. 67 N.C. 278 (1872).

13. *Id.* at 279.

14. *See., e.g.,* Lloyd v. Town of Venable, 168 N.C. 531, 533, 84 S.E. 855, 856 (1915) ("But in all those cases provision had been made for condemnation, including compensation. It was, therefore, very correctly held that the remedy of the statute was exclusive; but when no such remedy is given, the landowner, where property has been taken for the laying out of streets, may resort to his common-law action for compensation; otherwise, he would be without remedy").

local government inverse condemnation have had a statutory procedure available to them that encompasses the various alternative approaches previously employed by the courts. In *McAdoo v. City of Greensboro*,[15] the North Carolina Court of Appeals said that "[t]he exclusive remedy for failure to compensate for a 'taking' is inverse condemnation under G.S. 40A-51," thereby barring claims in trespass.[16] The court also said that "[t]he fact that G.S. 40A-51(c) provides that '[n]othing in this action shall in any manner affect an owner's common-law right to bring an action in tort for damage to his property' is not relevant" because an owner has no common law trespass action against a city.[17] The court of appeals later interpreted G.S. 40A-51(c) as preserving claims an owner might have in connection with specific damage from negligence, rather than recovery for general loss of property value.[18]

In several cases the North Carolina Supreme Court held that an owner had a right to bring a claim in court for compensation for an appropriation of property when the owner had not complied with a special procedure for claims against the alleged condemnor. In *Mason v. Durham County*,[19] the court held that an owner could pursue a claim to compensation in court in connection with a road widening despite not having followed a statutory procedure for submitting a request to the county commissioners for compensation when the county had denied that the owner had any property that was taken.[20] Shortly after *Mason* the court held that an owner of land abutting a street could bring a court action without having complied with a city charter requirement for submission of the claim to a city-appointed administrative board when the city had denied the owner was entitled to any compensation in connection with a change in grade.[21] A few years later, in *Rouse v. City of Kinston*,[22] the court held that an owner could bring a claim for compensation in connection with

---

15. 91 N.C. App. 570, 372 S.E.2d 742 (1988).

16. *Id.* at 573, 372 S.E.2d at 744; *see also* T-Wol Acquisition Co. v. Housing Auth. of the City of Durham, No. COA05-143, 2006 N.C. App. LEXIS 430 (N.C. Ct. App. Feb. 21, 2006) (no trespass claim against housing authority); Central Carolina Developers v. Moore Water & Sewer Auth., 148 N.C. App. 564, 559 S.E.2d 230 (2002) (remedy under G.S. 40A-51 is exclusive; no trespass claim against water and sewer authority).

17. *McAdoo*, 91 N.C. App. at 573, 372 S.E.2d at 744.

18. Howell v. City of Lumberton, 144 N.C. App. 695, 699–702, 548 S.E.2d 835, 838–40 (2001).

19. 175 N.C. 638, 96 S.E. 110 (1918).

20. *Id.* at 642, 96 S.E. at 112.

21. Keener v. City of Asheville, 177 N.C. 1, 4, 97 S.E. 724, 725–26 (1919).

22. 188 N.C. 1, 123 S.E. 482 (1924).

the city's installation of wells for its water supply, which the owner said had depleted his plantation's artesian wells, when the city had denied that the owner had any compensable ownership rights.[23] The court later described *Mason* and the cases following it as involving requirements for petitions to boards that had ministerial functions, and the court said that in those cases "there was a denial of title, making it necessary for plaintiff to resort to the Superior Court for a determination of the question of ownership and the right to claim damages."[24] Similarly in a later case the court held that an owner could bring an action in court for a determination of property rights and for compensation if such rights were found to exist, notwithstanding a city charter procedure for a condemnation claim, when the city had denied that the owner had compensable ownership rights.[25] These issues should not arise in a claim against a local condemnor with eminent domain authority under Chapter 40A, because the Chapter 40A procedure affords the owner an opportunity for resolution of disputes about ownership and compensable property rights.

4.2.2 Time Limit

Payment of compensation for property taken by the government is a constitutional mandate, but the General Assembly may define the requisite procedure for landowners to make a claim for the required compensation. A claim against a local public condemnor with eminent domain authority under Chapter 40A must comply with the statute of limitations of G.S. 40A-51(a),[26] which is as follows: "The action may be initiated within 24 months of the date of the taking of the affected property or the completion of the project involving the taking, whichever shall occur later."

If a public project has discrete subparts, the limitations period will be measured from when the effects of the subparts become apparent, rather than from when the overall project is commenced. In *McAdoo v. City of Greensboro*,[27] a road-widening project was completed in sections, with different contractors performing the work on the individual sections. The court of appeals, construing a statute of limitations period that began to run upon

---

23. *Id.*

24. Latham v. State Highway Comm'n, 191 N.C. 141, 143, 131 S.E. 385, 386–87 (1926).

25. Kistler v. City of Raleigh, 261 N.C. 775, 776, 136 S.E.2d 78, 80 (1964).

26. Smith v. City of Charlotte, 79 N.C. App. 517, 339 S.E.2d 844 (1986).

27. 91 N.C. App. 570, 372 S.E.2d 742 (1988).

"the completion of the project" involving the taking, held that each individual section could be deemed a "project."[28]

As described in section 4.5 below, the courts have recognized that certain kinds of restrictive regulations can be a basis for an inverse condemnation claim. In these circumstances the statute of limitations will begin to run when the ordinance is adopted. The owner is presumed to know of the impact at that time.[29] For instance, the court of appeals held that the limitations period for inverse condemnation as a result of a restrictive sign ordinance began to run when the ordinance was adopted, not later when the owner's sign would have to be removed after expiration of the period during which noncompliant signs could continue to be maintained.[30]

If in a rare circumstance an owner were to have a claim for compensation against a condemnor for which no procedure is available under Chapter 40A, the claim would be subject to procedural requirements for civil actions generally, as well as subject to the limitations periods that apply to the particular claims being made. The limitation period for an action for continuing trespass is specified in G.S. 1-52(3), which is three years from when the original trespass occurred.[31] The limitation period for physical damage to property is specified in G.S. 1-52(16), which requires that the action be filed within three years after the physical damage "becomes apparent or ought reasonably to have become apparent to the claimant, whichever event occurs first," but no later than ten years after the last act or omission on which the claim is based.[32]

As described in the next section, issues sometimes arise about whether the damage for which the owner seeks compensation was something for which the owner could have been expected to make a claim when an eminent domain procedure was available. As the discussion explains, the courts look at whether the owner could have foreseen the allegedly damaging conditions.

---

28. *Id.* at 572–73, 372 S.E.2d at 744 (construing G.S. 40A-51(a)).

29. G.S. 160A-364.1 provides that "[a] cause of action as to the validity of any zoning ordinance, or amendment thereto, adopted under this Article or other applicable law shall accrue upon adoption of the ordinance, or amendment thereto, and shall be brought within two months as provided in G.S. § 1-54.1."

30. Naegele Outdoor Adver. Inc. v. City of Winston-Salem, 113 N.C. App. 758, 440 S.E.2d 842 (1994).

31. Hoyle v. City of Charlotte, 276 N.C. 292, 307, 172 S.E.2d 1, 11 (1970).

32. *See* Robertson v. City of High Point, 129 N.C. App. 88, 497 S.E.2d 300 (1998) (discussing statutes of limitations).

4.2.3 Unforeseeable Conditions

The legislature authorizes an eminent domain procedure to enable public enterprises to acquire property needed for public improvements. Once the rights are acquired and compensation is paid, the matter of property rights should be settled and the owner cannot sue to prevent construction or continued operation of the improvement or for damages based on a claim that the compensation was insufficient. The eminent domain procedure is the appropriate forum to resolve all questions about the extent of the taking and the amount of compensation for the project and its operation, including claims by owners that the effect on their property rights is greater than the condemnor depicted in the eminent domain proceeding. If owners were able to bring repetitious claims, the public enterprise could be consumed with defending and paying compensation, which would defeat what the legislature was enabling when it authorized use of eminent domain by the enterprise. As the North Carolina Supreme Court has said, the condemnation proceeding is the place for the owner to make all claims for compensation in connection with the project for which the owner's property is taken, including "for all injuries to the remaining property, incidental to and necessarily resulting from the taking."[33]

Sometimes a public project causes harm that an owner could not reasonably have foreseen. In such circumstances the courts have focused on the unfairness of denying a remedy to an owner who could not reasonably have anticipated the effect of the public project when the government acquired the property for it. For example, in *Mullen v. Lake Drummond Canal & Water Co.*,[34] the owner's land was flooded by water from a canal, which inundated ditches the owner had maintained to catch anticipated overflow. Eminent domain had been used to acquire land for the canal's construction. The court rejected the canal company's claim that the condemnation foreclosed the plaintiff's claim for damages because "[i]t is well settled that no damages are contemplated in the original condemnation, except such as *necessarily* arise in the *proper* construction of the work."[35] In *Dayton v. City of Asheville*,[36] the North Carolina Supreme Court held that an owner's claim for compensation in connection with damage from smoke, grease, and ash from a city's

---

33. Ingram v. City of Hickory, 191 N.C. 48, 53, 131 S.E. 270, 273 (1926).
34. 130 N.C. 496, 41 S.E. 1027 (1902).
35. *Id.* at 503, 41 S.E. at 1030 (emphasis in original).
36. 185 N.C. 12, 115 S.E. 827 (1923).

garbage incinerator accrued when the first substantial injury occurred, not when the facility was first constructed if the harm was not yet occurring. [37] In *Hoyle v. City of Charlotte*,[38] the court held that a claim for compensation in connection with airplane traffic approaching an airport did not accrue until the flights became frequent and regular.[39] In *Midgett v. North Carolina State Highway Commission*,[40] the court held that the limitation period for seeking compensation in connection with drainage problems attributed to highway construction should be measured from when the damage occurred and became apparent, not necessarily when the project was completed.[41]

Although an owner may have a claim to compensation for damage that could not have been foreseen when the project was completed, the claim must be based on the project's impact, not on losses resulting from changes in surrounding conditions. The condemnation award need not anticipate the effects of later private development. In *Lea Co. v. North Carolina Board of Transportation*[42] the North Carolina Supreme Court considered an owner's claim in connection with flooding that the owner attributed to highway construction. The court said, "Injury properly may be found to be a foreseeable direct result of government structures when it is shown that the increased flooding causing the injury would have been the natural result of the structures *at the time their construction was undertaken*. Injury caused in substantial part by subsequent or contemporaneous acts or construction by others is not a direct result of the government structures. A showing of injury caused by such subsequent or contemporaneous acts or construction will not support a finding that there has been a taking by the State."[43]

When a public activity causes damage to an owner's property, the owner also may be entitled to recover damages in the same manner as anyone whose property is harmed by another's fault. For example, a condemnor's acquisition of easements for a sewer line will not foreclose an owner's later action for

---

37. *Id.* at 13–16, 115 S.E. at 828–29.

38. 276 N.C. 292, 172 S.E.2d 1 (1970).

39. *Id.* at 307–8, 172 S.E.2d at 11.

40. 260 N.C. 241, 132 S.E.2d 599 (1963).

41. *Id.* at 250–51, 132 S.E.2d at 608. The supreme court later affirmed dismissal of the landowner's claim, however, on the grounds that the state could not have anticipated the conditions about which the owner complained and the owner did not prove negligent construction or maintenance. Midgett v. North Carolina State Highway Comm'n, 265 N.C. 373, 144 S.E.2d 121 (1965).

42. 308 N.C. 603, 304 S.E.2d 164 (1983).

43. *Id.* at 617, 304 S.E.2d at 174 (emphasis in original).

negligent sewer maintenance.[44] Such claims are subject to the rules governing tort actions generally, including possible sovereign immunity and applicable statutes of limitations.

4.3 Inverse Condemnation for Physical Intrusions

Many local government activities have an impact on the neighborhood in which they are located. Incinerators, sewage plants, and prisons are among the most conspicuous examples of public activities that most owners do not want to have nearby. But roads, transmission lines, schools, and other common public improvements also affect the use and value of private properties. Many of these improvements enhance the value of the properties that enjoy their benefits, and to some degree all property owners benefit from the availability of public services. The law of inverse condemnation tries to distinguish between those public improvements that entitle owners to compensation and those that do not. The courts often have looked to trespass and nuisance principles to delineate this boundary.

A nuisance is an unreasonable interference with another person's use and enjoyment of that person's property.[45] An activity only becomes a nuisance as a result of its effect on its neighborhood. As the United States Supreme Court once put it, "A nuisance may be merely a right thing in the wrong place,—like a pig in the parlor instead of the barnyard."[46] For example, a use of property that generates so much noise that it unreasonably interferes with others' reasonable uses of their property could be a nuisance.[47] Something

---

44. Howell v. City of Lumberton, 144 N.C. App. 695, 548 S.E.2d 835 (2001).

45. Barrier v. Troutman, 231 N.C. 47, 49–50, 55 S.E.2d 923, 925 (1949).

46. Village of Euclid v. Ambler Realty Co., 272 U.S. 365, 388 (1926).

47. Hooks v. Int'l Speedways Inc., 263 N.C. 686, 690–91, 140 S.E.2d 387, 390–91 (1965). Such conditions also may be made criminal offenses by statute. G.S. 19-1. For a colorful description of the nuisance concept, see Carpenter v. Boyles, 213 N.C. 432, 450, 196 S.E. 850, 862 (1938) ("Centuries ago the Almighty entered a judgment, 'destruction by fire,' against two cities in the plain of the Jordan. Today the fire of the law must sometimes be applied by upright citizens to the Sodoms and Gomorrahs that have sprung up along our highways, creating nuisances against public morals").

that might ordinarily not be a nuisance can become one through negligent operation or maintenance. But an unreasonable interference with another's use of property need not be the result of negligence for it to be a nuisance, nor need the action causing the condition have been intentional.[48] When the condition unreasonably interferes with use of private property, compensation may be required. As the North Carolina Supreme Court said, "[T]he creation and maintenance of a governmental project so as to constitute a nuisance substantially impairing the value of private property, is, in a constitutional sense, a taking within the principle of eminent domain."[49] Although a nuisance condition may equate to a taking, the landowner's remedy is not an injunction as is normally available to the victims of nuisance.[50] Instead, the owner's remedy is compensation for the diminished property value, while the government may continue the activity that causes the nuisance.

In the leading case of *Long v. City of Charlotte*,[51] the North Carolina Supreme Court gave the following description of what all owners must tolerate within a community without reasonably expecting compensation: "Obviously, not every act or happening injurious to a landowner, his property, or his use thereof is compensable. Landowners must suffer the usual, normal and occasional disturbances, annoyances and discomforts of life such as a passing siren, a humming transformer or electric substation, the odor of a sewage treatment plant or paper mill 'when the wind is right,' a distant sonic boom or airplanes passing overhead."[52] Therefore, the "public importance and social utility" of various activities must be balanced against the inconvenience, annoyance, and aggravation to those in the vicinity.[53] As the court said, "This balancing of interests necessarily and properly places a heavy burden on the landowner."[54] The court further explained that "[t]he balance of interests is established by the requirement that in order to recover

---

48. Morgan v. High Penn Oil Co., 238 N.C. 185, 191–94, 77 S.E.2d 682, 687–90 (1953).

49. City of Raleigh v. Edwards, 235 N.C. 671, 674–75, 71 S.E.2d 396, 399 (1952).

50. Causby v. High Penn Oil Co., 244 N.C. 235, 93 S.E.2d 79 (1956) (discussing injunctions against nuisances).

51. 306 N.C. 187, 293 S.E.2d 101 (1982).

52. *Id.* at 199, 293 S.E.2d at 109.

53. *Id.* at 200, 293 S.E.2d at 110.

54. *Id.*

for the interference with one's property, the owner must establish not merely an occasional trespass or nuisance, but an interference substantial enough to reduce the market value of his property."[55]

One of the most common activities resulting in inverse condemnation claims is the operation of a sewage facility. In a number of cases, the North Carolina Supreme Court has found that compensation may be required when the characteristics of a sewage facility have a serious effect on particular property. In an early case, the court noted the public need for such facilities and the inappropriateness of injunctive relief to prevent their operation but also noted that "[t]his general principle is subject to the limitation that neither a municipal corporation nor other governmental agency is allowed to establish and maintain a nuisance, causing appreciable damage to the property of a private owner, without being liable for it. To the extent of the damage done to such property, it is regarded and dealt with as a taking or appropriation of the property, and it is well understood that such an interference with the rights of ownership may not be made or authorized except on compensation first made pursuant to the law of the land."[56] In *Clinard v. Town of Kernersville*,[57] the court held that damages may be appropriate as a result of polluting wastewater discharge from a sewage disposal plant.[58] The court said, "The pollution of a stream is equivalent to a taking and an appropriation in part. The law permits the acquisition of the easement in such cases by the payment of permanent damages, the judgment having that effect."[59] Courts also have employed nuisance concepts when considering owners' claims to compensation for persistently intrusive odors emitted from facilities such as sewage plants.[60]

The courts also have looked to trespass principles for determining when a government activity constitutes a taking. A trespass is intentional entry onto the property of another without permission or privilege.[61] A trespass

---

55. *Id.*

56. Hines v. City of Rocky Mount, 162 N.C. 409, 412, 78 S.E. 510, 511 (1913).

57. 215 N.C. 745, 3 S.E.2d 267 (1939).

58. *Id.* at 748–49, 3 S.E.2d at 270.

59. *Id.* at 749, 3 S.E.2d at 270 (citations omitted).

60. *E.g.,* Ingram v. City of Hickory, 191 N.C. 48, 131 S.E. 270 (1926) (sewage pipe discharged effluent onto the landowner's property, allegedly impairing the property's value because of fumes and odors).

61. Singleton v. Haywood Elec. Membership Corp., 357 N.C. 623, 627, 588 S.E.2d 871, 874 (2003).

is considered "continuous" if the intrusion is permanent in nature, as occurs when a structure is built on someone else's property.[62] A trespass also occurs when someone enters property with permission but then exceeds the express or implied authority. For example, an owner may be entitled to compensation for inverse condemnation if government uses its eminent domain authority to acquire a power line easement but then installs a road along the easement area. In *Phillips v. Postal Telegraph-Cable Co.*,[63] the North Carolina Supreme Court held that a landowner was entitled to damages when a telegraph company installed a line after acquiring an easement from a railroad with a right-of-way over the owner's property. The owner was not a party to the eminent domain action in which the telegraph company acquired rights to use the railroad right-of-way.[64] Although the owner's claim was based on trespass, the court referred to the constitutional nature of the owner's right to compensation.[65] The court said, "The Legislature may prescribe a form of procedure to be observed in the taking of private property for public use, but it is not due process of law if provision be not made for compensation."[66]

The courts sometimes have analyzed claims for property intrusions by government activities with reference to trespass, but in other instances merely have relied on the underlying notion of freedom from uninvited and uncompensated property intrusions. In an early railroad case, a landowner challenged the railroad's use of a public street over which the city held an easement for a highway use.[67] The North Carolina Supreme Court held that "use of a street for steam railroads is not a legitimate use of the street for public purposes" and that the landowner could sue for damages resulting from this expanded use.[68] The court instructed that "the plaintiff may maintain a common law action for damages, to be assessed up to the time of the trial, or it seems she may sue for the permanent damage, if any, which has been inflicted upon her property by reason of the location and construction of the defendant's road, and by so doing confer upon the defendant (so far as she

---

62. *Id.*

63. 130 N.C. 513, 41 S.E. 1022 (1902).

64. *Id.* at 523–24, 41 S.E. at 1025.

65. *Id.* at 521, 41 S.E. at 1024–25.

66. *Id.* at 521, 41 S.E. at 1024.

67. White v. Northwestern North Carolina R.R., 113 N.C. 610, 18 S.E. 330 (1893).

68. *Id.* at 617, 18 S.E. at 332.

is concerned) an easement to occupy the street."[69] The court referred to the action only as one at common law while employing a trespass analysis.

A few years later, the court considered a claim by a landowner for damages alleged to have been caused to crops by water collection resulting from railroad construction.[70] The court instructed that the construction of a railroad authorized by law could not be a nuisance, but that a landowner may bring an action for a "permanent appropriation."[71] The court reasoned that a single damage award was appropriate in exchange for the right to continue the operation, to protect those who exercise eminent domain powers for public purposes from "continual annoyance by suits" for operation of the improvement.[72] The court said that "[t]he measure of damage is the difference in the value of the plaintiff's land with the railway constructed as it is, and what would have been its value had the road been skillfully constructed."[73]

Urban development has brought with it government activities having a more obviously intensive impact on the surrounding environment than previously experienced, and the courts have had to reconcile the need for such activities with owners' rights to compensation for intrusions having an especially negative effect on their properties. The cases have held that although the activity cannot be prevented, compensation might be required. In the 1923 case of *Dayton v. City of Asheville*,[74] a landowner brought an action in trespass for smoke, grease, and ash coming onto the owner's land from a municipal garbage incinerator.[75] The court said that a city properly operating the facility could have no liability in trespass: "Indeed, the city having a right to erect the incinerator and to maintain it for the benefit of the public, in the exercise of a governmental duty, it will not be held civilly liable to individuals for injuries resulting therefrom, when properly built and operated, upon the theory of a trespass, in the absence of some legislative authority or a statute conferring such right of action."[76] The court also said, however, that "the denial of a right to recover against a municipality for an alleged injury upon the theory of its constituting a trespass does not militate against the right of

---

69. *Id.* at 622, 18 S.E. at 334.
70. Ridley v. Seaboard and Roanoke R.R., 118 N.C. 996, 24 S.E. 730 (1896).
71. *Id.* at 1000–1009, 24 S.E. at 731–35.
72. *Id.* at 1005–6, 24 S.E. at 733.
73. *Id.* at 1009–10, 24 S.E. at 735.
74. 185 N.C. 12, 115 S.E. 827 (1923).
75. *Id.* at 13, 115 S.E. at 828.
76. *Id.* at 15, 115 S.E. at 828.

recovery for a taking or appropriating, in whole or in part, of property for a public use without due compensation."[77] That is, "The alleged injury consists in the doing of a lawful act, but in such a manner as to amount to a partial taking of the property in question for a public use."[78] As the North Carolina Supreme Court later explained, "Unless made so by statute, a government agency is not liable for the torts and wrongs of its employees and agents in the performance of its duties for the public benefit. But if a governmental agency maintains a nuisance, permanent in nature, causing damage to and diminution in the value of land, the nuisance is regarded and dealt with as an appropriation of property to the extent of the injury inflicted."[79]

An owner's entitlement to compensation on an inverse condemnation theory is based on the permanent effect of the intrusion on the value of the owner's property. The North Carolina Supreme Court described the circumstances under which a taking occurs as follows: "'Taking' under the power of eminent domain may be defined generally as entering upon private property for more than a momentary period and, under the warrant or color of legal authority, devoting it to a public use, or otherwise informally appropriating or injuriously affecting it in such a way as substantially to oust the owner and deprive him of all beneficial enjoyment thereof.'"[80] As the court explained in 1914 in *Rhodes v. City of Durham*,[81] "where the injuries are by reason of structures or conditions permanent in their nature, and their existence and maintenance is guaranteed or protected by the power of eminent domain or because the interest of the public therein is of such an exigent nature that right of abatement at the instance of an individual is of necessity denied, it is open to either plaintiff or defendant to demand that permanent damages be awarded; the proceedings in such cases to some extent taking on the nature of condemning an easement."[82]

The balance of interests considered in the inverse condemnation analysis limits compensation to damage from ongoing conditions. In one of its earliest

---

77. *Id.* at 15, 115 S.E. at 828–29.

78. *Id.* at 15, 115 S.E. at 828.

79. Midgett v. North Carolina State Highway Comm'n, 260 N.C. 241, 247–48, 132 S.E.2d 599, 606 (1963) (citations omitted).

80. Ledford v. North Carolina State Highway Comm'n, 279 N.C. 188, 190–91, 181 S.E.2d 466, 468 (1971) (quoting 26 Am. Jur. 2d Eminent Domain § 157 (1966)).

81. 165 N.C. 679, 81 S.E. 938 (1914).

82. *Id.* at 680, 81 S.E. at 939.

decisions, the North Carolina Court of Appeals effectively summarized the approach to inverse condemnation claims with the following quote from a federal court opinion:

> "A compensable taking under the federal constitution, like the phrase 'just compensation' is not capable of precise definition. And the adjudicated cases have steered a rather uneven course between a tortious act for which the sovereign is immune except insofar as it has expressly consented to be liable, and those acts amounting to an imposition of a servitude for which the constitution implies a promise to justly compensate. Generally it is held that a single destructive act without a deliberate intent to assert or acquire a proprietary interest or dominion is tortious and within the rule of immunity."[83]

The court held that no taking occurred when a county sprayed insecticide that allegedly caused crop damage.[84]

As available land becomes ever more scarce and the demand for public improvements intensifies, the law of inverse condemnation must continue to evolve. This evolution occurs in a legal environment in which the courts have held that some expectations about protected property rights are not the subject of a compensation claim. For example, in reviewing an award of compensation for the effect of an environmentally hazardous material landfill on the plaintiffs' land, the court of appeals held that a reduction in market value as a result of the landfill was not a taking when there was no physical invasion of the property that interferes with its use.[85] The court of appeals also held that obstruction of a billboard by vegetation and trees planted for a highway beautification project was not compensable because the plantings did not directly interfere with or disturb the owner's property, and "the obscuring of plaintiff's billboards was only a consequential or incidental result" that was not compensable as a condemnation.[86]

---

83. Bynum v. Onslow County, 1 N.C. App. 351, 355, 161 S.E.2d 607, 610 (1968) (quoting Harris v. United States, 205 F.2d 765, 767 (10th Cir. 1953)).

84. *Bynum,* 1 N.C. App. at 356, 161 S.E.2d at 610.

85. Twitty v. North Carolina, 85 N.C. App. 42, 55, 354 S.E.2d 296, 304 (1987).

86. Adams Outdoor Adver. of Charlotte v. North Carolina Dep't of Transp., 112 N.C. App. 120, 123, 434 S.E.2d 666, 668 (1993).

A common issue involving an owner's claim to compensation involves tree trimming by government authorities. The North Carolina Supreme Court held that a government may trim and cut trees along a roadway in fulfilling its responsibility to maintain streets,[87] provided the work is done reasonably and in good faith.[88] A condemnor may trim or remove trees in connection with the installation or maintenance of a public improvement, but damage to or destruction of valuable trees may entitle the owner to compensation.[89] An encroachment that impedes travel is a nuisance and may be abated.[90] As the North Carolina Supreme Court said, "At common law any unnecessary or unauthorized obstruction that unreasonably incommodes or impedes the lawful use of a street or highway is a nuisance. These traveled ways must be made and kept in repair and made reasonably safe and convenient for the public. In the present day this duty is more incumbent, as the highways and streets are now used for quicker travel by truck and automobile, and obstructions are necessarily more dangerous."[91] But a landowner may have a claim to compensation if tree destruction or damage was not reasonably intended to protect the public.[92]

4.4 Inverse Condemnation for Changes Affecting Access

Local government eminent domain cases commonly involve road construction and expansion that affect the public road access of privately owned

---

87. Tate v. City of Greensboro, 114 N.C. 392, 19 S.E. 767 (1894).

88. Rosenthal v. City of Goldsboro, 149 N.C. 128, 62 S.E. 905 (1908).

89. *E.g.,* Moore v. Carolina Power & Light Co., 163 N.C. 300, 79 S.E. 596 (1913) (owner may be entitled to compensation when tree cutting reduces land's value).

90. Graham v. City of Charlotte, 186 N.C. 649, 120 S.E. 466 (1923); *see also* G.S. 153A-140 ("A county shall have authority, subject to the provisions of Article 57 of Chapter 106 of the General Statutes [regarding agricultural and forestry operations], to remove, abate, or remedy everything that is dangerous or prejudicial to the public health or safety"); G.S. 160A-193(a) ("A city shall have authority to summarily remove, abate, or remedy everything in the city limits, or within one mile thereof, that is dangerous or prejudicial to the public health or public safety").

91. *Graham*, 186 N.C. at 663–64, 120 S.E. at 473.

92. Rhyne v. Town of Mount Holly, 251 N.C. 521, 528, 112 S.E.2d 40, 46 (1960).

parcels. Such cases also involve the determination and payment of compensation when the market values of these parcels are diminished by changes that result in restricted access. Changes affecting access also are a common source of inverse condemnation claims.[93] The North Carolina Supreme Court has held that abutting landowners have a protected interest in road access. As the court explained, "It is generally recognized that the owner of land abutting a highway has a right beyond that which is enjoyed by the general public, a special right of easement in the public road for access purposes, and this is a property right which cannot be damaged or taken from him without due compensation."[94] Changes in road configuration can have a substantial effect on abutting properties, rendering them nearly worthless if the changes make access impossible or unreasonably difficult. In an early case, *Harper v. Town of Lenoir*,[95] the North Carolina Supreme Court affirmed an award of damages when changes in road grade resulted in a ledge that separated the owner's land from the road. The court said that compensation must be paid to the extent that the road construction diminished the value of the owner's premises.[96]

The North Carolina Supreme Court has said, however, that "'[a]n individual proprietor has no right to insist that the entire volume of traffic that would naturally flow over a highway of which he owns the fee pass undiverted and unobstructed.'"[97] As the court further explained, "To entitle a landowner to damages in the closing of a portion of a highway, he must show that he has suffered an injury different in kind from that suffered by the general public."[98] Also, an owner is not entitled to compensation merely because some of the

---

93. When a part of an owner's land is taken and road access is affected, the required compensation will include the diminished value of the affected land. Dep't of Transp. v. M.M. Fowler Inc., 361 N.C 1, 5, 637 S.E.2d 885, 889 (2006). Valuation issues are addressed in Chapter 3. This section considers the law governing whether inverse condemnation occurs when off-site changes are made to the road but no fee or easement in the owner's land is acquired through eminent domain.

94. Abdalla v. State Highway Comm'n, 261 N.C. 114, 118, 134 S.E.2d 81, 84 (1964).

95. 152 N.C. 723, 68 S.E. 228 (1910).

96. *Id.* at 725–30, 68 S.E. at 229–31.

97. Barnes v. North Carolina State Highway Comm'n, 257 N.C. 507, 515, 126 S.E.2d 732, 738 (1962) (quoting 2 NICHOLS ON EMINENT DOMAIN § 6.445 (3d ed)).

98. Snow v. North Carolina State Highway Comm'n, 262 N.C. 169, 173, 136 S.E.2d 678, 682 (1964).

passing traffic has been diminished by a change in configuration, because nearly every owner would be entitled to compensation whenever improvements were made to reduce hazards.[99] Access restrictions, median installation, and other changes that control travel can be undertaken pursuant to the police power in "the interest of public safety, convenience and general welfare"[100] without triggering any obligation to pay compensation for the common effect of such measures.

The availability of alternate access routes is a factor the courts consider when determining whether road changes have an impact on abutting property that requires compensation. The North Carolina Supreme Court has instructed that "where all direct access to a highway has been eliminated or substantially interfered with, causing diminution in value of an abutting property, the landowner is entitled to damages therefor."[101] On the other hand, the court has said that "[a]n abutting property owner is not entitled to compensation because of circuity of travel, so long as he has access to the highway which abuts his property."[102] Only a change that substantially impairs convenient access to the property is compensable unless a statute authorizes payment for less serious modifications.[103] Changes that limit a commercial site's access to travel over residential streets may warrant payment of compensation.[104] Compensation is based on the diminished value of the affected tract.[105] As the North Carolina Supreme Court noted, "The availability of alternative access and its reasonableness would be appropriate considerations in awarding damages."[106] Thus if the changed access configuration does not result in an appreciably diminished market value because alternative routes are sufficient to support the property's highest and best use, there will be no entitlement to compensation.

---

99. *Id.* at 174, 136 S.E.2d at 682.

100. *Id.* at 175, 136 S.E.2d at 683.

101. Dep't of Transp. v. Harkey, 308 N.C. 148, 154, 301 S.E.2d 64, 68 (1983).

102. *Snow*, 262 N.C. at 173–74, 136 S.E.2d at 682.

103. Abdalla v. State Highway Comm'n, 261 N.C. 114, 118, 134 S.E.2d 81, 84 (1964).

104. *Harkey*, 308 N.C. at 158, 301 S.E.2d at 70–71; Dr. T.C. Smith Co. v. North Carolina State Highway Comm'n, 279 N.C. 328, 334–36, 182 S.E.2d 383, 387–88 (1971).

105. *Dr. T.C. Smith Co.*, 279 N.C. at 335, 182 S.E.2d at 387.

106. *Harkey*, 308 N.C. at 158, 301 S.E.2d at 70–71.

4.5   Regulatory Takings

The government is deemed to have a "police power" to restrict property use to protect public health and safety. Owners' rights are subject to changes in regulations governing the nature and extent of permissible property uses. As a federal district court in North Carolina explained, "[A] reasonable property owner must expect that the uses of his property may be restricted from time to time by the state in the legitimate exercise of its police power."[107] As the court further explained, "A person who purchases land with notice of statutory impediments to the right to develop that land can justify few, if any, legitimate investment-backed expectations of development rights which rise to the level of constitutionally protected property rights. . . . [T]he state cannot be the guarantor by inverse condemnation proceedings, of the investment risk which people choose to take in the face of statutory or regulatory impediments."[108]

The impact from reasonable regulations therefore is not normally compensable, but the courts have held that regulations can be excessive. As land use regulations became commonplace in the twentieth century, a new type of eminent domain claim arose for "regulatory takings." Justice Holmes wrote the foundational opinion on regulatory takings in *Pennsylvania Coal Co. v. Mahon*,[109] in which the United States Supreme Court considered whether a taking occurred as a result of a Pennsylvania statute prohibiting mining that would cause the ground beneath a house to subside. In a now-famous phrase Justice Holmes said, "The general rule at least is, that while property may be regulated to a certain extent, if regulation goes too far it will be recognized as a taking."[110] He warned that if the Constitution's protection against taking private property without compensation "is found to be qualified by the police power, the natural tendency of human nature is to extend the qualification more and more until at last private property disappears."[111] A landowner therefore is entitled to compensation for a use deprivation that "goes too far." The difficult question is whether any particular regulation "goes too far."

---

107. Naegele Outdoor Adver. Inc. v. City of Durham, 803 F. Supp. 1068, 1079 (M.D.N.C. 1992).

108. *Id.* (quoting Claridge v. New Hampshire Wetlands Bd., 485 A.2d 287, 291 (N.H. 1984)).

109. 260 U.S. 393 (1922).

110. *Id.* at 415.

111. *Id.*

All land use regulations affect property values to some degree, and the United States Supreme Court has noted that courts "uniformly reject the proposition that diminution in property value, standing alone, can establish a 'taking.'"[112] In general the courts have expanded the notion of permissible regulations as local governments have perceived more need to address harm from urbanization with land use controls.[113] Also, the courts have upheld the government's authority to enact land use regulations that protect the community from identifiable harm. As the United States Supreme Court said, "Long ago it was recognized that 'all property in this country is held under the implied obligation that the owner's use of it shall not be injurious to the community,' and the Takings Clause does not transform that principle to one that requires a compensation whenever the State asserts its power to enforce it."[114]

The next two sections describe the basic contours of the courts' struggle with regulatory takings, the first addressing cases based on the United States Constitution and the second addressing North Carolina state court opinions. The third section addresses cases concerning government exactions required in exchange for development approvals.

4.5.1 Regulatory Takings Based on the United States Constitution

Several United States Supreme Court cases have built a framework for making the difficult distinction between property restrictions that must be borne without compensation and those for which payment must be made. In *Penn Central Transportation Co. v. New York City*,[115] the Court held that a historic preservation regulation prohibiting construction of an office building on top of the Grand Central railroad terminal was not a taking because "[t]he restrictions imposed are substantially related to the promotion of the general welfare and not only permit reasonable beneficial use of the landmark site but also

---

112. Penn Central Transp. Co. v. New York City, 438 U.S. 104, 131 (1978).

113. *See* Village of Euclid v. Ambler Realty Co., 272 U.S. 365, 387 (1926) ("Regulations, the wisdom, necessity and validity of which, as applied to existing conditions, are so apparent that they are now uniformly sustained, a century ago, or even half a century ago, probably would have been rejected as arbitrary and oppressive").

114. Keystone Bituminous Coal Ass'n v. DeBenedictis, 480 U.S. 470, 491–92 (1987) (quoting Mugler v. Kansas, 123 U.S. 623, 665 (1887)) (citations omitted).

115. 438 U.S. 104 (1978).

afford [the owner] opportunities further to enhance not only the Terminal site property but also other properties."[116] The Supreme Court later described its approach as requiring consideration of "a complex of factors including the regulation's economic effect on the landowner, the extent to which the regulation interferes with reasonable investment-backed expectations, and the character of the government action."[117] In *First English Evangelical Lutheran Church of Glendale v. County of Los Angeles*[118] the Court held that a regulation prohibiting the construction or reconstruction of any building or structure in a flood protection area was a taking. The Court said that its "cases reflect the fact that 'temporary' takings which, as here, deny a landowner all use of his property, are not different in kind from permanent takings, for which the Constitution clearly requires compensation."[119] In *Lucas v. South Carolina Coastal Council*[120] the Court held that a prohibition against building within a designated coast area unconstitutionally denied a lot owner property without compensation. The Court said that a taking occurs when a regulation "declares 'off-limits' all economically productive or beneficial uses of land."[121] The Court held that although government may enact regulations to address a harmful land use, mere legislative "recitation of a noxious-use justification cannot be the basis for departing from our categorical rule that total regulatory takings must be compensated. If it were, departure would virtually always be allowed."[122] In *Tahoe–Sierra Preservation Council Inc. v. Tahoe Regional Planning Agency*,[123] however, the Court held that a thirty-two month moratorium on development in the Lake Tahoe Basin did not offend the Court's sense of "fairness and justice" for limitations imposed on property owners. The Court said it would not attempt to devise a general rule about when a moratorium on development would be excessive and suggested that such a limitation could be developed by a state's legislature.[124]

The Supreme Court therefore has held that there are limits to the ability of government to prohibit use of property without paying compensation to

---

116. *Id.* at 138.
117. Palazzolo v. Rhode Island, 533 U.S. 606, 617 (2001).
118. 482 U.S. 304 (1987).
119. *Id.* at 318.
120. 505 U.S. 1003 (1992).
121. *Id.* at 1030.
122. *Id.* at 1026.
123. 535 U.S. 302 (2002).
124. *Id.* at 334–43.

owners. But the cases do not provide a clear measure of those limits, and the outcome can turn on particular justices' sense of "fairness and justice."

4.5.2 North Carolina Law on Regulatory Takings

As discussed above, the Supreme Court cases give some guideposts about the required analysis for determining whether a regulation constitutes a taking of property without compensation under the United States Constitution, but these cases provide no templates. The North Carolina Supreme Court's opinions reflect the same approach to determining whether a regulation is a taking under the federal or state constitution. The state supreme court explained its general approach to determining whether a land use restriction is excessive as follows: "First, is the object of the legislation within the scope of the police power? Second, considering all the surrounding circumstances and particular facts of the case is the means by which the governmental entity has chosen to regulate reasonable?"[125] The court's analysis of what is "reasonable" has reflected the same kinds of general concepts expressed by the United States Supreme Court. In *Helms v. City of Charlotte*[126] the North Carolina Supreme Court followed an approach similar to what the United States Supreme Court employed in *Lucas,* as described above, stating that "'[a] zoning of land for residential purposes is unreasonable and confiscatory and therefore illegal where it is practically impossible to use the land in question for residential purposes.'"[127] But the North Carolina Supreme Court held that a city acted within its police powers when it enacted regulations placing conditions on construction in an area designated as susceptible to flooding, relying on *Penn Central* in concluding that such restrictions were in the legitimate public interest.[128]

---

125. A-S-P Associates v. City of Raleigh, 298 N.C. 207, 214, 258 S.E.2d 444, 448–49 (1979) (citations omitted).

126. 255 N.C. 647, 122 S.E.2d 817 (1961).

127. *Id.* at 653, 122 S.E.2d at 822 (quoting 8 McQuillin, Municipal Corporations § 25.45, at 104–5).

128. Responsible Citizens in Opposition to the Flood Plain Ordinance v. City of Asheville, 308 N.C. 255, 266–67, 302 S.E.2d 204, 211–12 (1983); *see also, e.g.,* Weeks v. North Carolina Dep't of Natural Resources and Cmty. Dev., 97 N.C. App. 215, 388 S.E.2d 228 (1990) (denial of a pier permit was not a taking when the restriction protected public rights and interest, a shorter pier might be allowed, and other property uses were retained); JWL Investments Inc. v. Gilford County Bd. of Adjustment, 133 N.C. App. 426, 515 S.E.2d 715 (1999) (scenic corridor ordinance

To determine whether a regulation requires compensation, North Carolina courts also look at both the purpose and effect of the regulation. The North Carolina Supreme Court described the factors for determining whether a particular restriction goes beyond the constitutionally permissible extent of the police power as follows:

> In short, then, the court is to engage in an "ends-means" analysis in deciding whether a particular exercise of the police power is legitimate. The court first determines whether the ends sought, *i.e.*, the object of the legislation, is within the scope of the power. The court then determines whether the means chosen to regulate are reasonable. Justice Brock stated that this second inquiry is really a "two-pronged" test. That is, in determining if the means chosen are reasonable the court must answer the following: "(1) Is the statute in its application reasonably necessary to promote the accomplishment of a public good and (2) is the interference with the owner's right to use his property as he deems appropriate reasonable in degree?"[129]

In the court's landmark decision of *Responsible Citizens in Opposition to the Flood Plain Ordinance v. City of Asheville*,[130] the court held that development restrictions on land in a flood hazard district were a legitimate and reasonable use of the police power for the public good.[131] The court instructed that the police power analysis is intertwined with the question of when a regulation constitutes a taking because an excessive regulation will likely result in a taking without compensation.[132] The court said that conditional affirmative duties for new construction were analogous to the landmark preservation regulations held constitutional in *Penn Central*.[133]

---

that prohibits outdoor vehicle storage yard does not deprive the landowner of all economically beneficial use).

129. *Responsible Citizens*, 308 N.C. at 261–62, 302 S.E.2d at 208 (quoting *A-S-P Associates*, 298 N.C. at 214, 258 S.E.2d at 449).

130. 308 N.C. 255, 302 S.E.2d 204 (1983).

131. *Id.* at 262–63, 302 S.E.2d at 209.

132. *See id.* at 263, 302 S.E.2d at 209 (invalid land use regulation that unreasonably interferes with exercise of property rights "in effect constitutes a 'taking' of the owner's land").

133. *Id.* at 266–67, 302 S.E.2d at 211–12.

Shortly after *Responsible Citizens*, in *Finch v. City of Durham*[134] the opinions of a divided state supreme court demonstrated the difficult analysis necessary when a land use regulation borders on being a permissible exercise of the police power. A municipality rezoned a parcel to prevent commercial uses while the plaintiffs held an option to purchase the property they said they intended to develop for a hotel. The plaintiffs claimed the rezoning left the property with only potential uses that were not economically viable. A profitable residential development was not feasible because the necessary multi-lot development would require construction of a cost-prohibitive subdivision road, and other limited noncommercial uses were unlikely to attract a buyer. A majority of the court said, "In short, the test for determining whether a taking has occurred in the context of a rezoning is whether the property as rezoned has a practical use and a reasonable value."[135] The majority analyzed the evidence and said it was not persuaded that the result of the rezoning met this standard; it found the plaintiffs' expert testimony about potential markets inconclusive, noting the absence of aggressive attempts to sell the property or to enhance development possibilities, and saw the plaintiffs' actions after the rezoning as "speculative." A dissenting opinion viewed the case differently and would have affirmed the trial judge's opinion "that the rezoning had deprived plaintiffs all *practical* uses of the property so that it had no *reasonable* value."[136] These differing views illustrate that the concepts involved in the regulatory taking analysis are subject to varying interpretations.

Some government activities that may diminish property values have been held not to be takings because the activities were deemed not to be sufficiently physically connected to the affected property. In *Twitty v. State of North Carolina*,[137] the court of appeals held that a taking occurs only when the government activity interferes with property use, as would be the case with a nuisance at common law. The court said that the mere presence of a government facility alleged to have diminished property values in the area is not a condemnation. The alleged harmful government activity in *Twitty* was the construction and operation of a landfill for toxic waste.[138] Similarly, the mere threat of eminent domain has been held not to be a

---

134. 325 N.C. 352, 384 S.E.2d 8 (1989).

135. *Id.* at 364, 384 S.E.2d at 15.

136. *Id.* at 376, 386, 384 S.E.2d 21, 26 (Exum, C.J., dissenting) (emphasis in original).

137. 85 N.C. App. 42, 354 S.E.2d 296 (1987).

138. *Id.* at 49–56, 354 S.E.2d at 301–5.

taking. In *Penn v. Carolina Virginia Coastal Corp.*,[139] landowners sought compensation for diminished property value they said was due to proposed highway construction. The court said, "But it appears that petitioners have, in athletic parlance, 'jumped the gun,' that is, started this proceeding before their right to do so has accrued."[140] The court also said that a "threat to take" or "preliminary surveys" in anticipation of a taking "are insufficient to constitute a taking on which a cause of action for a taking would arise in favor of the owner of the land."[141]

The North Carolina Supreme Court also has drawn a "distinction between cases involving a permanent physical occupation and cases involving governmental action outside a person's property which results in consequential damages."[142] In *Stillings v. City of Winston-Salem*,[143] the court held that no taking occurred when a city terminated waste collection franchises after annexing territories subject to the franchises. The court quoted this formulation from the United States Supreme Court's opinion in *Loretto v. Teleprompter Manhattan CATV Corp.*:[144] "[R]esolving whether public action works a taking is ordinarily an ad hoc inquiry in which several factors are particularly significant—the economic impact of the regulation, the extent to which it interferes with investment-backed expectations, and the character of the governmental action."[145] The court based its conclusion on an implicit statutory condition that the authority underlying the agreements would terminate if the areas were annexed, on an implied covenant that franchises were held subject to the municipality's police power, and on a view that municipal competition with the franchisees for the services did not entitle the franchisees to compensation.[146]

4.5.3 Exactions

Exactions are conditions placed on a development requiring the owner to dedicate property for public use, build public improvements, or pay fees toward public expenses such as road construction, schools, or parks. In two

---

139. 231 N.C. 481, 57 S.E.2d 817 (1950).

140. *Id.* at 484, 57 S.E.2d at 819.

141. *Id.* at 485, 57 S.E.2d at 820.

142. Stillings v. City of Winston-Salem, 311 N.C. 689, 697, 319 S.E.2d 233, 239 (1984).

143. 311 N.C. 689, 319 S.E.2d 233 (1984).

144. 458 U.S. 419 (1982).

145. *Id.* at 432 (quoted in *Stillings*, 311 N.C. at 698, 319 S.E.2d at 239).

146. *Stillings*, 311 N.C. at 696–98, 319 S.E.2d at 238–39.

cases the United States Supreme Court outlined a test for determining when an exaction may be demanded without infringing the constitutional prohibition against the taking of property without compensation. First, there must be a sufficient "nexus" between "legitimate state interests" and the government's exaction.[147] Second, if the required nexus exists, there must be "rough proportionality" between the exaction and the proposed development's projected impact.[148] The government has the burden to prove such proportionality.[149] "[N]o precise mathematical calculation is required," but the government must make "some sort of individualized determination" that the exaction "is related both in nature and extent to the impact of the proposed development."[150] These requirements are reflected in North Carolina statutes authorizing land use regulators to require contributions for roads based on a measure of the additional "trips generated from the subdivision or development."[151]

The few reported North Carolina cases involving exactions have not expounded on the analysis outlined by the United States Supreme Court. In *River Birch Associates v. City of Raleigh*,[152] the North Carolina Supreme Court applied the nexus requirement and held that an open space requirement for planning approval was a valid exercise of the police power. The court held that "[a] requirement of dedication of park space for subdivision approval does not necessarily constitute a taking. Where the subdivider creates the specific need for the parks, it is not unreasonable to charge the subdivider with the burden of providing them."[153] In *Batch v. Town of Chapel Hill*,[154] the court of appeals applied a rational nexus test and struck down a town requirement that an owner proposing a subdivision dedicate land for a town parkway. The court held that the parkway requirement was not sufficiently related to the proposed development's impact and that there was no showing of a commensurate benefit to the landowner in exchange for the demanded dedication.[155]

---

147. Nollan v. California Coastal Comm'n, 483 U.S. 825, 837 (1987).

148. Dolan v. City of Tigard, 512 U.S. 374, 391 (1994).

149. *Id.*

150. *Id.*

151. G.S. 153A-331(c) (counties); G.S. 160A-372(c) (municipalities).

152. 326 N.C. 100, 388 S.E.2d 538 (1990).

153. *Id.* at 122, 388 S.E. 2d at 551 (citation omitted).

154. 92 N.C. App. 601, 376 S.E.2d 22 (1989), *rev'd on other grounds*, 336 N.C. 1, 387 S.E.2d 655 (1990).

155. *Id.* at 620–22, 376 S.E.2d at 34–35.

.

Index

abandonment of project, 2.9

answer to complaint, 2.8.7

attorneys' fees awards, 2.11

commissioners, 2.3.2.1, 2.8.10

    commissioners' report, 2.8.11

    notice of appeal from commissioners' report, 2.8.12

compensation, owner's right, 1.4

complaint, declaration of taking, and notice of deposit, 2.8.3

consent judgments, 2.10

costs, recovering, 2.11

deposit, 2.8.3, 2.8.9

discovery, 2.7

dispute resolution forum, 2.3

    alternative dispute resolution, 2.3.1

    commissioners, 2.3.2.1

    court, 2.3.2.2

    jury, 2.3.2.2

    litigation, 2.3.2

eminent domain authority

    coastal counties and municipalities, 1.7.4

    community college trustees, 1.8.1

    counties, 1.7.1, 1.7.3, 1.7.4

    federal housing projects, 1.8.2

    hospital authorities, 1.8.3

    housing authorities, 1.8.4

    joint municipal electrical power projects, 1.9.1

eminent domain authority, *continued*
    local acts, 1.10
    mosquito control districts, 1.8.5
    municipalities, 1.7.1, 1.7.2, 1.7.4
    public landings, 1.9.2
    public transportation authorities, 1.9.3
    regional natural gas districts, 1.9.4
    regional public transportation authorities, 1.8.6
    regional solid waste management authorities, 1.9.5
    revenue bond projects, 1.9.6
    sanitary district boards, 1.8.7
    school boards, 1.8.8
    special airport districts, 1.9.7
    state highway system streets, 1.9.8
    urban redevelopment commissions, 1.8.9
    water and sewer local government organizations, 1.8.10
eminent domain power
    cross-jurisdictional, 1.11
    nature of, 1.1
    origins of, 1.2
evidence, 2.7
exactions, 4.5.3
expert witnesses, 2.7
fair market value, 3.1
guardians ad litem, 2.6.2
injunctions, 2.5.3
interest on compensation, 3.14
inverse condemnation
    access, changes affecting, 4.4
    exactions, 4.5.3
    exclusivity of statutory procedure, 4.2.1
    intrusions, 4.3
    limitations periods, 4.2.2
    origins and nature, 4.1
    procedure, 2.13, 4.2
    regulatory takings, 4.5
    time limits, 4.2.2
    unforeseeable conditions, 4.2.3

judgment, 2.10

juries, 2.3.2.2, 2.8.12

lis pendens, 2.8.5

memorandum of action, 2.8.5

notice of action, 2.8.2

notice of intent to enter property, 2.8.1

offer to purchase or request for gift, 2.2

owner's reacquisition of property taken, 2.9

partial takings, compensation for, 3.4, 3.5

parties to eminent domain action, 2.6

plat, 2.8.6

procedure, overview and practice considerations, 2.1

proof of property value, 2.7

property acquired, authority to determine, 1.6

public use and benefit, 1.3
>   court review of legislative authorization, 1.3.3
>   North Carolina law, 1.3.2
>   United States Supreme Court cases, 1.3.1

quick take, 2.5.1

register of deeds filings, 2.8.5, 2.10

regulatory takings, 4.5

relocation assistance, 3.13

reply to answer, 2.8.8

return of condemned property, 2.12

rights subject to eminent domain, 1.5

rules of litigation procedure, 2.4

summons and service, 2.8.4

takings without following procedure, *see* inverse condemnation

title to property taken, 2.5

unities, for determining property affected, 3.6

valuation, 3.2
>   affected property, 3.6
>   business income, 3.8
>   cost approach, 3.2.3
>   date as to which value is measured, 3.3
>   easements, 3.9
>   extraction rights, 3.7

valuation, *continued*

    income approach, 3.2.2

    interest on compensation, 3.14

    leases, 3.10

    liens, 3.12

    life estates, 3.11

    market comparison approach, 3.2.1

    partial takings, 3.4

    public improvements, effect of, 3.5

    relocation assistance, 3.13

    several interests, 3.7

vesting of title, 2.5

witnesses, 2.7